3491D   Pub at   1.5

C000205796

THE
ALTERNATIVE
HOLIDAY GUIDE
TO

Deep Sea
Fishing
around Europe

THE ALTERNATIVE HOLIDAY GUIDE TO

Deep Sea Fishing around Europe

by

Graeme Pullen

Ashford Press Publishing
Southampton
1988

Published by Ashford Press Publishing 1988
1 Church Road
Shedfield
Hampshire SO3 2HW

British Library Cataloguing in Publication Data

Pullen, Graeme
    The alternative holiday guide to deep
    sea fishing around Europe.
    1. Saltwater fishing – Europe –
    Handbooks, manuals, etc.
    I. Title
    799.1'6'094   SH603

    ISBN 1-85253-072-3

Designed and set by Jordan and Jordan, Fareham, Hampshire

Printed and bound by Robert Hartnoll (1985) Ltd., Bodmin, Cornwall

*To those footloose fishermen who search
for the greener grass. The search is often
more exciting than the discovery!*

Acknowledgements

The author and publisher gratefully acknowledge the valuable assistance from the following organisations in producing this title:

Irish Tourist Board; The Gambia National Tourist Office; Portuguese National Tourist Office; Spanish National Tourist Office.

Contents

List of Photographs

List of Maps

Introduction

The basic aim of any good book should be to either instruct or entertain the reader. Nothing is worse than a bored reader, so I have endeavoured through the pages within to marry together a little of the two. Rather than give a completely cold, factual list of contacts, I thought it better for anybody wishing to plan a trip to learn of the points that will interest him or her, and hopefully be of the greatest help. Travelling as much as I do, I have found over the years that I take less and less on trips, as it becomes clear that travelling to virtually anywhere involves much the same problems. You need a passport, an air ticket, and of course some form of cash or currency. With those you can at least do something constructive should you come across any hitches with hotels, bookings or civil problems. With just these three you can get home safely, but there are all those little extra tips that make the holiday one to remember and these you will find in the following pages.

This particular book has enabled me to pass on a little of my own experience involved in the world of foreign fishing, and while some writers are only interested in truly monster fish, I still have that yearning for catching anything of any size. Also, a small fish caught in difficult circumstances and from an area hitherto untried is so much more rewarding than just filling the boat with cod from British waters. But having had a few blank trips when I first started travelling abroad, I soon started to appreciate the value of local knowledge. The object of this book is not to tell you every single country where it is possible to go and catch fish. Some have too much pollution, some have absolutely no fishing facilities whatsoever. Others quite simply have not yet had their potential fully realised, so have no idea what is available for the touring angler to catch. I have included specific information only on those venues that I consider to be easy to reach, pleasant to stay at, and with a versatility and production of fishing that would make a trip there both enjoyable, and exciting. While some countries can still only be reached comfortably by means of tour operators and package holidays, in most the yearning to get out on your own, off the well beaten tourist trail, and do your own thing can be fulfilled. You can then see how the local people really live rather than watch the cultural entertainment laid on by many package companies. However, some of the package deals are very reasonably priced, and if that's the way to get somewhere then use it. The leading tour operators usually have couriers to assist with any transportation and travel enquiries, which does of course make you feel more at home.

Foreign countries invariably have warmer temperatures and sunnier skies than ours, but remember they too must have bad weather sometimes. Booking a holiday abroad and in advance is still very much a throw-of-the-dice affair, for you have no absolute guarantee of sunshine and blue skies. What you are doing is taking the better odds that the farther south you travel from our green (but wet) and pleasant land, the better the chance of sunshine. There will inevitably be some species of fish that I have missed out in this book, which is, after all, only intended as a general guide. But the fish I have named are definitely high on the list of encounters should you decide to take the plunge and book a day afloat. The primary target species I would aim for if I had to finalise a list for each country would be as follows, and I would consider myself a little unlucky if I failed to come up with the goods:

The west coast of Ireland – Tope, Pollock and Wrasse.
Algarve – Mullet.
Madeira – Tuna and Wahoo.
Canary Islands – Stingray, Marlin, and Bonito.
Azores – Atlantic Blue Marlin, Big Eye Tuna, and Blue and Mako sharks.
The Gambia – Ladyfish, Barracuda and Snapper.
Greece – Albacore and Mullet.

The beauty of foreign fishing is not just the pleasant climate, but the fact that you never really know just what is going to come up and grab your bait or lure. It may be big, it may be small, but it may be something you have never even seen before.

As well as giving you tips on the different species, there are tips on restaurants, wines, tours, places of interest, in fact many of those little things you don't find out until you get home. This guide will give that bit of extra information before you go, or may even fire your imagination, and get you rushing for the travel agents and those glossy brochures. The world of Sportfishing is expanding all the time as more and more people try their hand at what in the Stone Age was a necessity, i.e. feeding ourselves by catching fish. You may think you are simply going on holiday, but once you pick up that fishing rod, you are awakening an instinct to hunt that is dormant in most people all their lives. Fishing can unlock that door to the past, and satisfy a need that is all too quickly being lost with the advancement of modern society.

THE
AZORES

THE AZORES ARCHIPELAGO

CORVO

FLORES
LAJES

SAO JORGE
VS DAS VELAS

GRACIOSA

FAIAL
HORTA

PICO
LAJES

TERCEIRA
ANGRA DO
HEROISMO

SAO MIGUEL
PONTA
DELGADA

SANTA MARIA
VS DO PORTO

Travel Tips

Access

Of all the European venues I suggest in this book for the adventuring fisherman to try, none will set the pulse racing more than the Azores. Reputed to be part of the lost city of Atlantis, these islands were discovered by Portuguese navigators on their way to the New World. The sailors that stopped there named the islands after the hawks that circled the islands, which they mistook for vultures.

Reaching some of the more out of the way places is always slightly tedious. It would be nice to step on a plane at home and step straight out onto a fishing boat on landing. However, good fishing spots are not always that convenient, so access to the Azores is best undertaken as a whole day, or even two day affair. From the UK either book on a charter flight if available or for security of booking take a scheduled flight through TAP-Air Portugal, from Heathrow to Lisbon, on the Portuguese mainland. Here you can either take a connecting flight to Ponta Delgada on the main island of Sao Miguel that same day, or take an overnight in Lisbon and fly out the next day. If you leave the UK on an early morning flight then I suggest you make the TAP connection to Sao Miguel that same day. At least that way you get there reasonably quickly. If you have to overnight in Lisbon there are plenty of hotels to choose from, and taxis are available right outside the airport arrivals areas.

If you want to spend your entire trip on Sao Miguel everything is fine, but if you want to tour the whole archipelago you can either take a boat, which is very time consuming, or take the local airline SATA. SATA is the lifeblood of the islands' tourist economy and is a small airline serving the outer islands of Santa Maria, Terceira and Faial. Once on the main island of Sao Miguel there are always taxis around, and on the outer islands travel is best done by walking, bus or local taxi. Once on the island of Faial, you can take a short boat excursion across the bay to Pico, where stands a tremendous mountain, dominating the skyline to the south.

Health

Immigration require no visas for entry into the Azores, as you will have passed through Lisbon as your first port of entry, and been cleared at customs there. No special vaccination regulations are in force, although if you have passed through a foreign country with an epidemic you must have a certificate of vaccination. From the UK you merely require a valid British passport.

Accommodation

There are many hotels and apartments on the island of Sao Miguel, plus various small hotels on the islands of Faial, Santa Maria, and Terceira. Sao Miguel hotels have bars and a discotheque, plus there is a casino. There are also limited discotheques on the other islands, with the main one at Faial. The electricity is 220v 50 cycles using continental two pin plugs. The tap water is safe to drink, and bottled mineral water is available everywhere.

Money & Shopping

For those interested in shopping the local handicraft includes the rare art of scrimshaw, pieces of whalebone carved into items of beauty and interest. They also make wickerwork, hats, clogs, cane furniture, earthernware, beautiful needlepoint lace and delicate carvings made from fig pith. The banks in the islands are open 08.30–11.45, and 13.00–14.45, Monday to Friday. The currency is escudos.

Food

Local restaurants abound, especially on the islands of Sao Miguel, Faial and Pico, the cuisine of the islands being rich and varied. There are numerous fish dishes, and it is best to take the waiter's advice on the dish of the day, as the supply of fresh fish in these rich ocean waters is virtually endless. They have meats and cheeses, which when washed down with the famous Verdelho wine of Pico and Graciosa, make a meal an adventure in itself. Some of the local specialities that are worth trying are as follow:

Lapas a' molho Alfonso – these are limpets in a special sauce;
Alcatra a'moda da Terceira – a spicy beef casserole;
Linguica com inhames – a spicy sausage.

When on Sao Miguel you can sample the very latest in volcano cooking, when at Furnas, the cooking pots are buried in the ground and the food is slowly cooked by the sulphorous springs. The archipelago produces several fruits, the best to try being passion fruit, washed down with a pineapple liquer or angelica dessert wine.

The Islands

The archipelago consists of nine islands in the mid Atlantic, and less than two hours flying time from Lisbon, on mainland Portugal. With a total area of 2335 square kilometres the eastern group is Santa Maria, and Sao Miguel. The central group is Terceira, Graciosa, Sao Jorge, Pico and Faial, and the western group consists of Flores and Corvo.

Literally every one of these islands have the most fantastic fishing potential imaginable and in my opinion is the most underdeveloped potential in the modern fishing world. The volcanic structure of the archipelago has created the high inland lakes, the extinct craters and those ominous looking volcanic cones that are now so verdantly green. The climate creates this luxurious undergrowth of vegetation and riot of wild flowers, tempered by the islands' position on the latitude, and the regulating influence of the Gulfstream. The mean air temperature for the year is 17°C, with a maximum of 21, and a minimum of 14. The atmosphere, free from pollution, allows the amateur and professional photographer to snap away merrily. Tones are enhanced by the changing clouds, and the rays of the sun change Pico especially, from a bland silhouette to a plaster moulding of prehistoric times. Many of the high pressure weather systems start here, known as the Azores anticyclone belt. The wind, considering it has the entire north Atlantic to race over unhindered, is only some 12.2km per hour. Ideal for the sailing enthusiast, (the islands are used as provisioning points by trans-Atlantic sailors) and ideal, of course, for fishing. The weather changes very quickly. It can rain and blow in the morning, then be still with a clear blue sky in the evenings.

The combination of these natural conditions allows a prolific growth of vegetation, which, as well as interesting native species that are elsewhere extinct, includes various exotic plants and trees from all over the world. Game is still abundant. Buzzards, that gave the islands their name, still visit the islands. Livestock breeding is now one of the mainstays of the islanders, which together with the agriculture, wines and other industries makes tourism a joy. Unspoiled by pollution, and unravaged by the commercialism of the rest of Europe, these islands really are one of the few places left in the world where you can get away from it all. According to the 1970 census there is a resident population of 287,000. Many years ago the Nova Scotia whaling boats would stop in the Azores to take on men, as the locals were among the finest, and most fearless whalers of the day, with a reputation for reliability that preceded them worldwide. Looking at the islands separately they all have something unique to commend them.

Sao Miguel

Sao Miguel is usually the first that most anglers see on landing at Ponta Delgada. This is the operational base of the local airline

The author took a British party of anglers to Faial Island at the end of the fishing season in October. Many said they would never catch. But of course they did. In just five days' fishing with artificial lures, they landed 9 blue marlin to 762 lbs, 2 bigeye tuna to 175 lbs, and long to return. Here the boat is backed as an angler bends into a billfish.

SATA, and Ponta Delgada is the largest town in the group. Full of 18th-century history, it has everything to keep a fisherman and his family interested as they explore some of the areas, such as Caldeira das Sete Cidades. A gigantic, extinct crater, with an area of about 40 square kilometres, with two lakes joined by a causeway bridge. One lake is an emerald green. The other a deep blue. As well as being unusual it is full of fish, all freshwater species, with the carp shoals taking bread, and the perch, reputed to weigh over 5 lbs, falling to a spinner. There are also other species including pike. I once had a phone call from a specialist carp fisherman who assured me he had information that the lakes held massive carp over 60 lbs. As yet I have heard of nobody catching one, but for the sake of aquiring a licence to fish, it is certainly worth spending a day here. The waters, nearly always sheltered from any wind by the high crater walls, reflect the beautiful hydrangeas and ruches, making the whole crater a suntrap when the sun is high. According to legend, one of the seven cities of Atlantis was submerged in this crater. I don't know about that, but I certainly would like to find the whereabouts of some of those carp!

Riberia Grande is a tea plantation area with a black lava plateau, and hot sulphurous springs. Lagoa da Fogo is an immense extinct crater containing a lake filled with crystal clear water. Pico do Ferro – an area of steaming springs, waterfalls, lush vegetation and palm trees. The thermal spa water is of great value in the shape of the many geysers, fumaroles and medicinal mud. There is also a large hot natural water swimming pool, and various walks around the same area. Sao Miguel probably has the most tourist attractions of all the islands and at least a couple of days is needed away from the fishing to really take them all in.

Faial Island

Faial Island is without doubt the best for big game fishing, hosting several gameboats albeit very expensive. The fishing is for big marlin and tuna. I had the privilege of being the first person to ever take a pair of marlin from this island, and since that historic occasion there has been an influx of boats and great numbers of marlin caught. The boat prices have risen to a high level, due mainly to the superb fishing, which is a great shame because many Europeans will be unable to afford the prices. There is an

A historic photograph. The author was the first angler ever to land a marlin on a rod and line from the island of Faial. He did it in style, taking this pair of blue marlin using Murray Brothers' lures, on 23rd August 1985.

airport which is served by SATA and a large port at Horta with regular ocean and coastal services. The island gets its name from the profusion of beech forests that covered it when it was first discovered. The fields have an amazing border of beautiful hydrangeas, making wavy blue lines up the mountainside in a fretwork of colour. Tuna fishing and whaling were the primary sources of commerce, and while the whaling has finished, the commercial pole fishermen still work the area for the vast shoals of tuna that swim there. Local handicrafts include straw embrodiery and rope, lace, objects made from hydrangea stems, flowers made of fish scales and shells, objects made from cachalot bone, and the usual embroidery and basketwork. The town of Horta overlooks the bay and the other island of Pico, and the view from the hill overlooking the town is well worth the taxi ride. The Church of Sao Francisco has 17th-century paintings, and there is a religous art museum. Caldeira, the highest crater rim on the island, is over 3000 feet above sea level and is covered with luxurious vegetation. It is now a reserve, and has that heady strange silence of a vast open-roofed cathedral. Now it looks beautiful with lush greens, but it takes little imagination to realise the wrath it must have expended during its days of power. At Capelinhos, Ponta Furada and Lajinha there are villages that have actually been made from the volcanic rock, and are surrounded by contrasting fields of golden corn. At Castelo Blanco, a noted mark showing the start of the marlin grounds is a huge flat topped basaltic rock, thrusting from the sea, while at Varadouro there is a beach of basaltic sand and hot springs. The whole island of Faial has cliffs and rocks that drop to the deep water, and when the sun shines it would be hard to find a more peaceful place. In a storm, the wild Atlantic lashes those same rocks with untold fury, creating the amazing architecture of nature we see today.

Pico Island

Just a few miles across the water from Horta harbour on Faial rises the majestic mountain of Pico. Over 7000 feet high, it is the highest in Portugal and is used by the local fishermen to tell what the following day's weather is going to be like. If he 'has his moustache on', a thread of cumulous cutting the peak about midway, the weather will deteriorate. How often I have found that to be true. There is an aerodrome and the port is famous for being the master port for open-boat whaling until quite recently. It has strange volcanic formations, constrasted even from Faial when the sun drops low in the westering sky. They are called locally 'mysterios', these black lava outcrops with strange forms. The wine of Pico is famous, and I have a few friends who testify to both the hospitality of the Pico people, and the strength of the verdelho wine! Forests of chestnut and pine trees alternate with the hydrangeas and mimosas, making a climb up the mountain an exhilarating experience. Farm implements and straw hats are the local handicrafts. Faial can be reached by the daily ferry and taxis are available for people wanting to visit there just for the day. Other items of interest for the touring angler are: a church made of black lava; the whaling museum, surely a must for fishermen on a rainy day; a grotto with stalagmites at Furna fe Frei Matias; a small village by the sea at Sao Rogue, at the foot of a verdant slope, and some interesting lakes at Madalena which I believe are supposed to hold black bass and carp.

Sao Jorge Island

This has an aerodrome and is linked by the inter-island coastal services. It is a long narrow strip of land, with steep slopes down to the sea, and pasturage enclosed by hedges of hydrangeas and cedars. This is a livestock area with supplementary produce in the shape of dairy produce, fruit and fishing. The local coloured rugs of linen and wool and the embroidered quilts are prized collector's items. At Velas, there is a 17th-century church, and the other points of interest are Furnas das Pombas, the lovely lakes of Fajas and Caldeira, and Pico da Esperanca. Many of the islands in this archipelago have species of plants that are rare, while some are even extinct in other places in the world, so look but try not to pick them.

Graciosa Island

This also has an aerodrome with a port in the process of construction. It is served by the inter-island coastal services, and has something of a rustic charm with cultivated fields and flowers. Some of the chapels command panoramic views, particularly from Monte de Ajuda. At Furna do Enxofre there is a deep crater with an underground lake. There are the Carapacho hot springs and the island has a spattering of windmills. Another of the islands that has tremendous big game fishing potential as a base from which to explore the fish-rich waters, yet so far nobody has started a charter boat operation there.

Terceira Island

This has a large international airport, which has links with both Canada and America, handling all kinds of aircraft especially military. It is used as the base for all the inter-island connecting flights of SATA, and the port is served with regular inter-island coastal services. The coastline is host to many sandy beaches and islets, while livestock and dairy produce is the mainstay of the island economy. There are two famous local wines, the 'Biscoitos' and 'Porto Martins' which are well worth trying if you stay there. Angro do Heroismo is the oldest town in the Azores, dating back to 1534, with its fine planning, and architectural balance. There are many churches to visit, and at Monte Brasil there are superb views and sea caves. At Sao Mateus there is a small fishing village from which it may be possible to hire a local boatman and craft to take you out exploring the many reefs and banks that make the bottom fishing so interesting. Panoramic views are seen from the top of Caldeira de Santa Barbara, some 3100 feet high, and both Sao Jorge and Graciosa can be seen from here, nestling on the horizon.

Flores Island

This is very small, but has an aerodrome and the usual boat service between the other islands. There is a small ocean port under construction. The name of the island comes from the many flowers that grow in profusion, even in the rugged terrain. Small extinct craters are everywhere, seven of which form lakes which hold a good number of trout, perch and carp. For cultivation the islanders grow cereals, bananas and oranges, which coupled to the livestock breeding, dairy produce and fishing, ensure a comfortable living. The weather can be kind around this island and there is good shore fishing potential from any of the rocks. At Santa Cruz there is an 18th-century church.

Corvo Island

This is the smallest island in the archipelago, with only a few hundred inhabitants that devote themselves to farming, cattle and fishing. There are special local customs, and even this island, as small as it is, has a crater with a lake – Caldeirao. It is an island apart from the others with the true living conditions of a pastoral and fishing community. Ideal for the shore angler who just wants to explore the shore fishing grounds.

The Fishing

Shore Fishing

Every one of these islands has a rugged, rocky coastline that is ideally suited to the angler wanting to scramble around and discover his own paradise pool on the edge of the ocean. There really are no hotspot marks to put you on to. It is more a case of taking a rod, a knapsack and a packed lunch, then exploring any area that takes your fancy.

Should you not wish to climb too far for your fish, and are staying on the main island of Sao Miguel, you could do worse than stay on the pier at Ponta Delgada. From here you can fish in the shelter of the harbour for a wide variety of small fish on light tackle, attracting them to your hookbait by helpings of local bread sopped up with some water and crushed sardine. You can buy some sardines from either the local fishermen or the market. Throw in a handful every few minutes and using polaroids and a wide brimmed hat to keep out the glare, stare into the water to see what comes along. Very often small mullet will be the first to arrive, and you can take these on freshwater tackle of light rod, 2 lb line and a size 16 freshwater hook. A piece of prawn/shrimp or bread will suffice for hookbait. By stepping up the line strength to 5/8 lbs, and using a bigger hook, say a size 2 freshwater, you can hit some of the local jacks and bream up to about 4 lbs that are attracted by the feeding frenzy of all the small fish. Evening or early morning is the best time for these. Bait should be a strip of squid or half a sardine. A leader of 15 lb mono may be needed.

Then again if you want something a bit larger, you simply walk along to the end of the pier and throw out either a fillet or fresh caught fish, a whole fresh fish or a couple of sardines on heavier shore tackle, 12 lb line, 12in wire trace and 2/0 hook, leaving it on the bottom. The stingrays will probably be the predominant species to take this and should weigh between 10 and 30 lbs, quite a handful from a pier. At night, a bass/cod-like fish moves into the harbour and may be caught using the same tackle and techniques. They are reputed to give a tremendous fight, and reach in excess of 30 lbs in weight. Nobody really knows exactly what can be caught from this pier, but there is no question that fishing with a big fresh bait legered on the bottom, yields big fish.

If you want something else to do at night you can lower a fillet of fish down the side of the harbour wall for some of the moray eels that live there. Of all the species of fish I have caught, a moray eel is the one I dislike most. They have tremendous jaw power, with a couple of fang-like teeth at the front of the mouth. Exercise care when unhooking, preferably pacifying first with a piece of 4 by 2 timber! On the north of the island there are also good rock marks for bluefish, a game scrapping species that run to about 8 lbs, and generally hit a spoon or livebait.

Casting into the deep water out from the cliff rocks is good for a wide variety of fish, and the bigger bluefish are more likely to hit on a flood tide in the evening. This rough ground will also give a mixed bag of bottom fish, but be prepared to lose a bit of tackle in the snags. I find it best to use stones or nuts and bolts as expendable weights when approaching such rough ground. Take care fishing these rocks in rough weather, as the swell from the Atlantic can rise up many feet. The local taxi drivers often know the best spots, and you can arrange with them what time to drop you off and collect you. Some, if fishermen themselves, will even stay with you throughout the day!

On the pier at Horta in Faial, you might also wish to try the shore fishing. Exactly the same techniques apply as with Sao Miguel, except the harbour wall is smaller, and the water not quite so deep. Stingrays come right up to where the fish are offloaded by the commercial tuna boats, presumably attracted by the smell of the decks being hosed down. There are thousands of small fish which can either be regarded as bait or sport, depending on how you wish to tackle the fishing. In amongst these are some species of jacks that run to maybe four pounds, and they seem only to hit small livebait at last light. I think a flashing spoon may also do the trick in the hours of darkness, as all jacks have excellent eyesight and may see the leader during daylight hours. I have never heard of the cod/bass-type species caught in Sao Miguel being caught here, but certainly the stingrays go to over 40 lbs in weight, and perhaps a good deal more. I would suggest a night session or two spent in search of the bigger rays, with a nice fresh fillet of fish legered on the bottom.

Much of the fishing you will do is experimental. The locals fish with bamboo poles for tiny fish using a bread paste for bait. Therefore there is little or no information about marks and availability of species. If at all possible I would buy as many sardines as you can and break them up with a mixture of bread, soaking it in a bucket or container, maybe mixing in some sand to make it sink quicker. Mould this into balls and throw it out into your chosen fishing area for a day or two prior to fishing. Squeeze the balls hard to prevent them breaking up too much on impact with the water. Then when you fish you should attract several different species in your area, which will be used to the feed you are throwing in.

Boat fishing

For boat fishing, the main charter boat company is run by *Pescatur*, and owned by Mr. Francisco Van Uden. There are two distinct seasons, and two distinct venues. From March to July the boats are usually based at Ponta Delgada on Sao Miguel where they fish for the big eye tuna. Then from August until November they are moved to Faial where they concentrate on the marlin and broadbill swordfish. The basic charter boats run by *Pescatur* are the Pacemakers. About 30 feet in length, they are powered by twin diesel engines and capable of twelve knots comfortably, 15 or 16

All action aboard the *Pescatur* gameboat *Rabao* as a big marlin is about to be released.

when flat out. Trolling speeds with artificial lures are between 8 and 10 knots. They come fully equipped with fishing tackle, fighting chairs, outriggers, echo sounder and safety equipment and lures.

According to Mr. Van Uden, the species season runs as follows: swordfish, white and blue marlin – August, September, October, November. Albacore and bigeye tuna runs are best during the months of April, May, June and July. The yellowfin tuna and big bluefin tuna run April, May, June and July, although in Faial in November 1986, the gameboat *Double Header* successfully landed a 700 lb (or more) bluefin tuna on rod and line. Most of the shark species, namely mako, hammerhead, blue, six gilled and whitetip are present all season, while the white sharks are present in February and March. Other species include bonito, skipjack tuna, dolphin (fish, not mammal), amberjack, horse eye jack, weakfish, bluefish, conger eel, and tope.

The boats take four fishermen plus two observers and can travel up to 50 miles from port. The maximum day's fishing is 9 hours, though generally it is 8. *Pescatur* have taken many European records for a wide variety of species, and once they start to learn the new marlin techniques they will surely be getting some more. My discovery of the marlin fishing on Faial island was a fortunate part of my angling career. Fishing on the *Pescatur* boat *Rabao* with Captain Luis Laje I hooked, in just five days' fishing, twenty marlin, breaking none off, but landing six. In addition, I had five mako sharks, two blue sharks and some dolphin. Needless to say my last day fishing – hooking no less than seven blue marlin and landing three – set the marlin world alight, and soon anglers were flocking to fish there. The truth is the fish had always been there, and I could just as easily have caught them had the boat been based at Sao Jorge or Pico island. The water all around here has an abundance of baitfish in the shape of vast skipjack tuna shoals, so it was really the fact that I was the first angler with any real knowledge of modern trolling techniques, which led to this haul. Since then a couple of top American boats have moved in, the best being *Double Header* and *Bandit*. Captain Chuck Tedder on the *Bandit* released over 80 blue marlin in the 1986 season alone, while Captain Don Merton on the *Double Header* took the rod and line European broadbill swordfish and bluefin tuna in November of the same year.

The local commercial fishermen were all quietly amazed by the amount of interest being shown in a species of fish that they knew to be present, but which had no commercial value. Yet here were crazy anglers wanting to catch a fish with little or no value, and pay vast sums of money for the privilege of doing so! In Horta, Faial lies a commercial tuna boat called *Geralda*. She drifted the banks off Sao Miguel once and took a staggering 34 broadbill swordfish, many over 300 lbs, in one night alone, plus large yellowfin and bigeye tuna in excess of 250 lbs. To top it off they boated eight big sharks. It was a wonder the boat still floated with that load aboard! In late 1986 a commercial tuna boat landed 24 bigeye tuna in just four hours fishing with livebait, while a *Pescatur* gameboat, complete with anglers who were risking a trip in the winter months, landed a 700 lb blue marlin, lost three other marlin, and boated six bigeye tuna... all in one day. So far from the island of Faial, the largest Atlantic blue marlin boated was landed by Leo Schaffer who took the 924 lb fish on a 80 lb line and a lure from a *Pescatur* boat. I myself couldn't get a booking until October 1986, when I fished with three other anglers. Using a variety of lures from Ed Murray we equalled the European record of five blue marlin in one day, the largest a 762 lb fish. In five days' fishing in unpredictable weather we landed no less than nine marlin and two bigeye tuna, and lost one mako shark. Another boat with English anglers aboard didn't have the same catch rate as us, but they still managed a few marlin, mostly from the *Double Header* with Captain Don Merton.

There are many good places to try around the islands, but in my experience four stand out above the others. The famous Condor bank is a good two hour steam from Horta on Faial, and is a plateau rising up from the ocean floor to create an upwelling of current and bait. The marlin in particular run the edge of this dropoff area, while the sharks, both mako and blue, are right on top of it.

The average size of the marlin is perhaps 300 lbs, which is very good, but I have heard one writer state an 'average' of 600 lbs, which of course taken over an entire season is a huge exaggeration. Many of these fish are released so it is easy to 'round up' the figures, and overestimate a fish in the water. The mako shark work out around 150 lbs average, although nobody knows just how big they grow, and with a 900 lb fish in Madeira, one can assume a fish of similar, if not larger proportions, is viable at any time in the bait-rich waters of the Azores. The blue shark run to over 400 lbs, and all-tackle records almost certainly exist, but again the average would be much lower, probably nearer

160 lbs each. The broadbill swordfish are very much an unknown quantity as far as sportfishing statistics go. Rather than give an average weight, I would suggest you can expect fish from 40 lbs to 100 lbs, then a jump to a bigger fish, somewhere around 300 lbs or so. The same goes for the bluefin tuna. With only one ever being landed on rod and line, at 792 lbs, you cannot derive an average. The day that fish was caught the *Double Header* also saw tuna to 1000 lbs, but could not fool them into taking. That tuna came from way out over the Azores bank, a major hotspot for white marlin, but a long run in a boat, and you need the weather to get there. I

A catch that many anglers only dream about. Graeme Pullen took this Atlantic blue marlin of 400 lbs, and mighty mako shark in the one day aboard *Rabao* skippered by Capt. Luis Laje. The author feels that Laje is the most instinctive fishing captain he has ever worked with.

have a feeling this bank could yield some huge bottom fish, with six-gilled shark and stone bass being among the bigger fish.

Bottom fishing with rod and line, hasn't even been touched. With the 250 fathom line so close to shore, there is a potential for taking marlin, tuna and shark from any of the three islands of Sao Jorge, Pico or Faial. However for big mako sharks you need fish from a drifting boat often no more than half a mile from shore. Sardines, which are easily purchased, and a couple of bonito bought from the freezer house will do you for baits. Fish with crushed sardines in a mesh bag hung from the side of the boat to attract a shark, and place your two baits, preferably both on 130 lb class tackle, with one bait deep, the other shallow. By shallow I mean twenty feet. By deep I mean a hundred feet deep, or even more. Trolling lures across towards Sao Jorge there is an area often frequented by very big blue marlin, in excess of 500 lbs, and it is here where I expect that first 1000 pounder to come from. The area is a long time favourite of the commercial tuna fisherman fishing bonito and bigeye, yet while most anglers specialising in big marlin think they are there to eat the skipjack tuna, I feel the really big marlin pick off small yellowfin tuna and bigeye tuna of 30 to 50 lbs.

Just off the tip of the south east of Faial there is a mark maybe a mile from shore. The mark is called Ribeirinho, and Leo Scaffer's 924 pounder came from here. Running along from here to the north-west, about one and a half miles offshore, you will notice a slanting rock formation, high at the right, low at the left. About level with the middle of the slope to the lower end is the hotspot where I hit seven in one day with Captain Luis Laje. It is an ideal spot when southerly and westerly winds put the Condor bank out of the question, as, provided you can sneak out of the harbour, it is possible to work this area all day with an excellent chance of a result. I have also taken both mako and blue shark here while drifting with rubby dubby. The immediate westerly tip of the island doesn't seem productive, but then nobody really tries in close here.

The blue marlin take artificial lures better than baits and this is due solely to the fact that a fast boat covers more ground than a slow boat and is therefore likely to find a cruising fish quicker. There will always be the odd captain that specialises in bait fishing, but as a general rule a good lure fisherman will always outfish a good bait fisherman. The advantages of bait fishing is when in search of a true leviathan of a marlin. Slow trolling with a live 20 or 30 lb yellowfin may well be the way to catch that 1000 pounder, and you are more likely to attract the attention of a shoal of sharks, especially mako, which love to take a passing chunk out of a nicely tethered yellowfin. Having said that I have myself caught mako on a lure, and they seem to have a preference for the flathead Moldcrafts made by Frank Johnson. They were intended for marlin, but that doesn't stop the mako eating them too! Mako are the fastest of the shark species, and a 150 pounder has, over a short distance, a remarkable turn of speed. Perhaps fast trolling with a set pattern of really outsize lures might be the answer for that big fish, but then I have had 150 lb marlin on what I thought were very large lures. The best thing to do is get out there and just fish it. As far as the inshore trolling with light tackle and small lures is concerned, I don't believe it has been really tried successfully yet. There are good bluefish to be caught by slow trolling along the coast with the larger size rapala magnum lures, plus the chance of bigger European barracuda. If you fished flatheaded trolling lures of six inches or so, and fished them quite fast you should connect with a racing wahoo, but bait fished in conjunction with a downrigger is far better.

The potential of these islands is almost endless, and in my mind will become *the* leading Big Game Fishing centre in the whole of Europe, possibly the entire Atlantic. For booking any of the *Pescatur* boats you should contact the following, as advance booking is always required if you want to book a boat:

Pescatur Big Game Fishing.
Mr. Francisco Van Uden,
Rua Joao Francisco Cabral,
40-D 1E.9500 Ponta Delgada.
Sao Miguel. Azores.
Tel: 22827.

There are several hotels and apartments on Faial, and one of the better speciality restaurants is the Club Naval, overlooking the harbour on the main street. It is always worth dropping in here for a drink as some of the charter skippers stop there for a beer, and you can learn what is being caught.

THE
CANARY ISLANDS

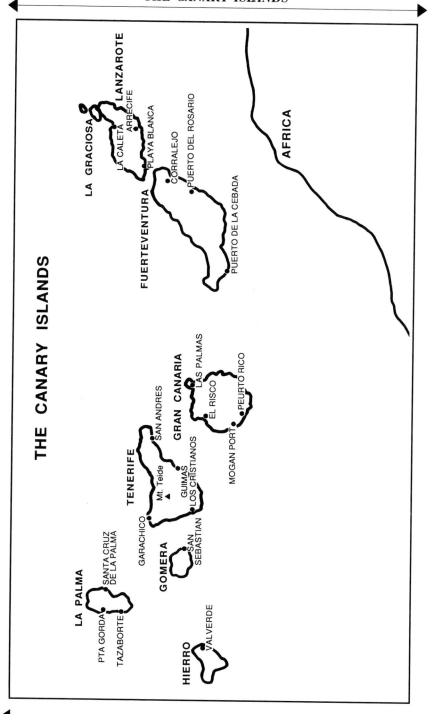

Travel Tips

Access

Getting to the Canary Islands is comparatively easy from Britain. Your local travel agent can offer you a multitude of different package companies from which to choose, and these offer air and usually ground transportation as well. This would be the cheapest and easiest way to reach the islands, which are situated just off the north-west coast of Africa. Most of the flights from the UK will be from Gatwick, Heathrow, Luton or Manchester airports, with Iberia offering a daily scheduled flight throughout the summer, and charter flights serviced by Air Europe, Brittania Airways, Dan-Air, Monarch and Cal-Air. Without a doubt the best airline I have travelled with is Air Europe, which has always supplied value for money and a first class service. The national daily newspapers also carry advertisements of reduced air fares from various companies, and one of the better companies I have travelled with is *Owners Abroad*, Valentine House, Ilford Hill, Ilford. Essex. It was created about fifteen years ago, and has grown from a small operation to be the second largest tour operator in the UK, now a public company under the heading *Owners Abroad Group plc.* They carry more than 100,000 passengers per year and are market leaders. In addition to facing the scrutiny of being a public company, it is licensed by the CAA and bonded for the financial security of its passengers. If a flight is available, you can use the computerised booking system with an Access or Visa card. Phone numbers for the national booking offices are as follows:

London: 01-514-4000.
Glasgow: 041-221-4681 or 041-221-6634.
Manchester: 061-834-7013.
Birmingham: 021-632-6723.

The best flights are from any of these four airports directly non-stop into the international airport of Las Palmas on Gran Canaria, the main island. I see no point in mentioning any of the cruise ships that dock for a day at Las Palmas, as most people want to get there quickly. A non-stop air flight takes a little under four hours to Las Palmas, depending on weather conditions en route, and density of European air traffic.

Health

The Canary Islands are owned by the Spanish and there are no specialised regulations regarding health or immigration in force. No innoculations are compulsory, and only a valid British passport is required for entry into the country. There is no worry about malarial carrying mosquitoes, though it is advisable to pack a small first aid kit in event of any minor injury or discomfort. A fully comprehensive medical insurance is advisable, covering delays, baggage loss, medical expenses etc. Your travel agent can advise you on this. If you wish to hire a car it is best to take your valid British driver's licence, and local insurance can be fully comprehensive when you book at the car hire office.

Ground Transportation

At Las Palmas airport on Gran Canaria island, there are taxis waiting just outside the arrival lounge. Most package companies have a representive who will meet you with a clipboard at the doorway to the arrival lounge, and should have transportation to your hotel organised. For touring, there are local tour companies that will advertise escorted tours in most of the larger resorts, or you can take the local bus service which travels quite frequently. The impressively clean black and green Mercedes taxis can always be found at the major resorts or hotels, or, should you want to get up in the mountains for a reasonable price, you can hire a car from one of the many companies in the major resorts.

Accommodation

While there are several islands in the Canaries, it is Gran Canaria that holds the interest for the sportfisherman. Therefore the accommodation centres would be confined to this area, and preferably within easy reach of the charter fleet. There are many hotels in the capital of Las Palmas, but this is situated in the north-east corner of the island, which is where the wind blows almost continually. The clouds build up from this area, so while it is warm, you may not actually see the sun for some time. My suggestion would be to get further south, below the shelter of the mountains, which is both closer to the charter fleet, and better for sunshine.

Two possibilities are Playa del Ingles and Maspalomas. Here there are plenty of hotels right on the beach, shops, restaurants and transportation services. It would probably take the best part of an hour by bus to get into Peurto Rico where the boats leave from. A taxi would be quicker but naturally more expensive. In Peurto Rico itself there are dozens of self catering apartments to choose from, all of which are set into the floor and walls of the surrounding valley. It is a modern development, and is continually being enlarged. For those who prefer something just a little quieter, there is the fishing village to the west of Peurto Rico called Mogan Port. Even so, this has had an extensive new marina recently built, together with new apartments, but it is still in its infancy and therefore very quiet when compared to Peurto Rico.

Communication

The islands are linked by both air and sea lines to Europe, Africa and America – the island closest to Africa is under 100 miles. Phoning the UK from say, Peurto Rico, is far cheaper by public payphone than it would be from a hotel, which surcharges any international calls.

The Islands

Centuries ago it was said that the Canary Islands were an arrival point for those who sailed off from the Mediterranean Sea, travelling south across the Hercules columns, finally reaching the archipelago. There are in fact seven islands here. Gran Canaria (Grand Canary), Lanzarote, Fuerteventura, Tenerife, La Palma, Gomera, and Hierro. There are also a few scattered, but uninhabited rocks and islands in the chain. These islands constitute the two most westerly provinces for Spain, on an average latitude which puts them near the northern boundary of the Tropic of Cancer. An alignment across the Atlantic would put that very roughly in line with Florida. The islands therefore have a sub-tropical climate due to the spring-like weather that prevails through the winter. Each island has its own distinctive geology and unique beauty. They were formed from the depths of the ocean

In contrast to the noise and heat of the coastal resorts, a trip up into the central mountain range of Gran Canaria is a refreshing change. The La Silla restaurant at Artenara just outside Tejeda is literally built into the side of the cliff, where you can dine on local food, sip the best wine and take in the most fantastic view. Even the most hardened fisherman enjoys a quiet day in the solitude of mountain scenery.

by a series of volcanic upheavals, a long process which is still in progress. They have mountain ranges with hidden peaks, shrouded by clouds, sandy deserts, abrupt rocky cliffs, perfectly formed craters and forests with lakes and reservoirs. It can be said that each island has a micro-climate of its own, and a history still quite young. Their origin is wrapped in legends woven about them by poets and Greek historians, resulting in the more popular name – 'The Fortunate Isles'. The ships of Columbus on their way to the discovery of America, stopped at Gomera and from there sailed off across what was then a mysterious ocean. The islands of today are a shopper's paradise as there is no customs barrier. Sometimes even the duty free shops at the airports have difficulty in competing with the plaza shops for products such as drink, cigarettes, electrical goods, watches or jewellery. Exotic buys are also to be had, whether a crocodile skin from Nigeria or real Chinese silk, these islands can often offer them at prices cheaper than in their country of origin.

There is good shore fishing to be had from any of the islands, and excellent potential for deep sea bluewater sport, limited only by the numbers of suitable craft. Many of the islands have small fishing villages, but the craft used are long wooden boats which are unsuitable and too slow for trolling for tuna and marlin.

Tenerife

At 1231 square miles, Tenerife is the largest in the chain, and is almost triangular in shape. It also has the highest point in Spain, that of Pico del Teide, some 12,270 feet high. Snow covered during the winter, it overlooks the equally impressive crater of Canadas del Teide, 12 miles in diameter and now designated a national park. Tenerife has a wide variety of flora, and cultivates bananas, tomatoes and potatoes. The capital of the island is Santa Cruz de Tenerife with 200,000 inhabitants, a city lying on the southern slope. The international airport of Reina Sofia is about 40 miles from Santa Cruz and Tenerife North is 5 1/2 miles away. Just over 13 miles from the capital is Mount Esperanza, with extensive forests of Canaries pine,which is crossed by a road leading to the Canadas del Teide,with lookout points giving impressive views of the island.

For the tourist angler there are several places of interest to visit, on the regular tours to villages of particular beauty or interest.

Try some of these if you have the time. For example, La Laguna, next most important centre to the capital; La Orotava which offers views, gardens and attractive churches; Puerto de la Cruz which is a tourist centre with good beaches, natural pools, good hotels and restaurants; Los Realejos, a setting of banana groves and farmland with some hotels. Icod, at the foot of Mt. Teide, is famous for its wines, which you should sample both on the way up and down the magnificent Teide. Garachico: once the most important port on the island with a beach of black sand indicative of the island's volcanic nature. Las Galletas: a sheltered beach beside the Lorenzo valley. Impressive views can be found at Punta Rasca, with tourist developments nearby. Arico is a clean town facing the peak of Guajara, with three beaches. Tacaronte is famous for its wines.

In the south of the island is the Hotel Playa Sur. Situated some 7km from the new International airport of Reina Sofia it is ideally located for an overnight stop. It is based on the only natural sand beach of the island, and is just a couple of minutes walk from the fishing village of El Medano. Whereas the north of Tenerife sees most of the rainfall, El Medano lies on the south side of the island where the air merges with the prevailing northerly winds to create moisture loss and thereby little rainfall. The hotel boasts a windsurfing school, as 75% of days end up with a strong wind blowing, often averaging Force 4–7. This is a good reason for taking care in the sun as burning is easier when a cooling breeze blows. The dry atmosphere is also excellent for asthma and breathing sufferers, with temperatures from 24/26 degrees Centigrade.

In October 1987 I was afforded the chance to test fish this area of Tenerife by the owner of the 95 foot gameboat *El Zorro*. Owner Jim Edmiston was on a two-year search for a record marlin, and collected myself and my wife from Tenerife to cruise down to the Cape Verde islands searching for new grounds. We fished from the smaller gameboat the *El Zorro Too*, captained by Florida fishing veteran Billy Borer. We were amazed by the pinnacle rock rising up from 500 metres, just a few miles out from the lighthouse to the north of El Medano. Here we recorded 300 feet of water only 150 yards from shore, with a tide rip boiling on the surface. We only had a short time fishing here, but both Billy and myself feel this is an area that truly big fish move through at certain times of the year. Well worth a look.

La Palma Island

This consists of 437 square miles and 76,000 inhabitants. A very green island, it has the largest known crater, now declared a national forest, at Caldera de Taburiente. It has a circumference of 17 miles and depths of as much as 2500 feet and is covered with immense pine forests. There is an Astro-physical Observatory at its highest point, some 8000 feet above sea level. The capital is Santa Cruz de la Palma, which lies on the eastern slope of the mountain. Places of interest for the holidaying fisherman would be as follows: Los Llanos de Aridane: the commercial and agricultural centre of the island, located in a valley. Tazacorte has banana groves, and also a small harbour and good beaches. Peurto de Naos is a small village, with a beach of fine black sand. Fuencaliente is the southernmost town on the island with pine groves and vineyards adjoining two volcanoes. Mazo: prehistoric inscriptions in the Belmaco Cave, and a good view over the surrounding coastline. San Andres y Sauces offers the Tilos forest, coves, clear waters and some gigantic ferns. Cueva Bonita has a beautiful natural grotto which is scoured out by the action of the sea.

Gomera

227 miles square and with 25,000 inhabitants, this island is almost circular in shape. Lush and leafy it has a national park which rises more than 4500 feet above sea level and is called Alto de Garajonay. To communicate between the mountains the islanders use a whistling technique which is now famous and unique to this island. It was here that Columbus made the final preparations to his ships before sailing to the Americas. Places of interest worth visiting are: Hermigua, with its white farms and rich banana plantations; El Bosque del Cedro, one of the most beautiful cedar groves in the islands; Vallehermoso, overlooked by the Organus rocks, with plantations of fruit trees, banana trees, palms, sabines, and an excellent beach; Playa Santiago, a small and quaint fishing village with clear waters lapping the beach and Valle Gran Rey which, with its palm groves, extensive banana grove and superb beach is one of the more popular stopping points on the island.

Hierro

This island is triangular in shape and lies at the extreme western end of the island group, the smallest of all the islands at 166 square miles. The capital is Valverde with some 5000 people, and is renowned for its beautiful orchards and gardens. At Peurto de la Estaca there is a church-fortress, and the airport is a few miles from the city. The mountains of the coast drop away abruptly into the sea, and much of the coastline is still covered with forest. Hierro island is ideal for the shore angler who wants to explore the rocks and coves with the minimum of disturbance. Of the interesting places to see while on the island, try the following. Frontera: the richest of the vineyard regions on the island, it lies close to Sabinosa which is renowned for its medicinal waters. To the south of the island is La Restinga, a place well worth a visit as the sea and underwater fishing is reputed to be the best on the island. El Tamaduste: crystal, calm waters form a large natural pool that is a pleasure to photograph in bright sunlight. Tinor: in the middle of the high meseta, it has pyramids of ashes in the surrounding green fields. Locally there are also some great views of the whole island, and remember that much of the geology is relatively new in formation.

Lanzarote

This is possibly one of the most barren in the group, almost as though it is still in the final stages of formation. Very volcanic, the scenery is vast and open, silent yet awesome. In times as recent as the 18th and 19th centuries there were vast volcanic eruptions which wiped out around 120 square miles and transformed the island into a fairly barren looking place. The capital of the island is Arrecife, a clean place overlooking the busy fishing port where stand the castles of San Roque and San Jose'. The beaches are at Reducto, Guacimeta and Playa Blanca. Between the airport and Peurto del Carmen there are also attractive beaches. The airport lies about three miles south of the capital.

With the harsh topography of the island, it really is amazing how the islanders manage to make an existence out of any form of agriculture. Yet by scooping out a hollow, filling it with fine volcanic ash, they can grow vines, melons, grapes, figs, tomatoes

An angler sweats it out in the noon sun as he fights a big marlin. The fisherman is Briton Chris Kent, who on his first ever trip to Peurto Rico with a group of anglers led by the author, hooked into a monster marlin estimated to weigh over 800 lbs. After a gruelling 2¼ hour fight the 80 lb line parted and the fish was gone. Such is fishing! The boat was the *Carmen* captained by Francisco.

and onions. Moisture is absorbed from overnight dew and this is sufficient for these plants to grow. Of tourist attractions there is the lava region of La Geria, the islet of Hilario, Montana fe Fuego, which is reached by camel back, and from which you can see around 300 volcanoes. The shore fishing can be quite good, but the angler will need light tackle and be prepared to walk along the beaches and coves, fishing as he goes, until he makes contact with a fish. Plenty of mullet can be seen and are taken by floatfishing with tiny pieces of bread. Groundbaiting with soaked bread will help bring them within reach.

Fuerteventura

This is the island with the longest coastline, immense beaches and a serenity for all those who wish to escape the pressures of modern life. It has a new airport with landing strip 8000 feet long suitable for national and international traffic through the day. The capital is Puerto Rosario, and even this has clean, long beaches.

Although Gran Canaria is the only island with a charter fleet operating, it is this long island that offers the best potential for new, exciting sport. Big tuna and marlin run the corridor between here and Africa, often chasing the sardine shoals passing in migration. The minimal tourism potential on this island is possibly the reason why nobody is operating a fleet of boats from here, but I would say once somebody started they would find some exciting sport. Dawn and dusk sessions along the beaches and rocky outcrops will give the enterprising angler the chance of a multitude of tiny reef fish, together with the ever present mullet shoals.

Graciosa Islet

This is separated from Fuerteventura by the narrow strait of El Rio. It is tiny in comparison, and has only 16$\frac{1}{2}$ square miles, with the maximum height at Montana de las Agujas of 907 feet above sea level. In the east is the harbour of Caleta del Sebo which is first class for both shore and sea fishing for reef fish. It has two notable beaches of fine golden sand at Las Conchas and Caleta del Sebo.

Gran Canaria

This is the island which the angler should go to for his first fishing sessions. It has some exciting shore fishing potential and some really good offshore deep sea sport. The methods of shore fishing here will apply to any of the other islands in the group, as similar species are likely to be caught. The charter fleet operate from Puerto Rico in the south, set in one of the many valleys and ravines that run down from the central mountain range down to

The south coast areas of Gran Canaria are starting to become built up, as the popularity of its superb weather gains momentum with the tourist industry. This totally new marina complex at Mogan Port has been tastefully designed to blend in with the background. It may also become a new base for a charter fishing fleet in the future.

the sea shore. Las Palmas, the capital, holds 350,000 inhabitants and therefore the heaviest traffic volume. Most airlines land at the airport here, and the city has many hotels, night clubs and an intense social life.

There are contrasting places up in the mountains and along the coast from Las Palmas, with desert areas and mountains with tropical vegetation. At Puerto de las Nieves the cliffs are near vertical, while the ravines of Tirajana, Moya and Azuaje are rugged, littered with distant valleys. In Agaete there are flourishing coffee trees, palm groves and banana plantations, almond trees, sugar cane and the vast tomato fields. At Las Canteras there is a magnificent beach over 1 1/2 miles long, with a temperature that is pleasant throughout the year. The winds generally blow from the north and are therefore split in two by the huge central mountain range which funnels them either side of the island to the east and the west. The very southern tip is almost always agreeably calm, which is why Peurto Rico is the hive of tourists you see today. There are two main ways to escape the packed beaches. To the south is the vast Atlantic, and to the north are the mountains.

Mogan Port to the west is less busy and well worth a visit, especially for lunch, and to the east lies Arguineguin, a small fishing village beside Point Percel. Both these spots being natural commercial fisheries offer the visiting angler a chance to sample the local caught fish, cooked in the traditional way. In Arguineguin try the Bar Marino, the old one overlooking the cement factory. It really is virtually full of locals, a sure indication that the food is good. Try as a starter the Potage and Rancho Canario, a sort of vegetable soup, and don't miss out on the Papas Arugadas and Mojo sauce. These are baby potatoes cooked in their skins, rolled in salt then dipped in a spicy garlic sauce. Very local and very tasty. Of the many and varied species of bottom fish worth trying the following are among the best: vieja is a steamed parrot fish; mero and cherne is grouper, a large flaky flesh with a dry flavour; gallo is the trigger fish which abounds in the deep water; breca, sama, busenegro are all in the bream family and the salema is a species of wrasse. There is another place overlooking the beach called Bar Marino Two, and this is also good, especially for octopus and squid. You can drop in later to the Bar Pino for a brandy with the locals.

At Mogan Port, one of the best restaurants is La Orilla del Mar run by Antonio. You may be lucky and hear some local guitar music as well. Try their hot grilled avocados. Up further into the valley you come to Mogan village – try the Tauro restaurant for guantaramo, a fresh fish and good meat mixture. They also are reputed to offer the best steak and chips on the island. If you really want to get completely away from it all you can hire a car from one of the many companies in the town of Peurto Rico, Mencey are as good as any, and drive right up into the mountains. They will direct you on a local map of the areas you can cover, but just below Mogan village there is a dirt track that takes you up into the mountains in a spectacular, winding, and perhaps dangerous fashion. It is a track used for jeep safaris, but I have taken a small Fiat panda hire car up there many times, and it really is an exciting drive. You aim for a mountain village called Tejeda, and after travelling through here you will come to a T-junction. You turn right towards Las Palmas but follow this road for only 300 yards before you take a concealed turning on your right at Artenara village to the La Silla restaurant. This small turning winds up to a car park clearing, from where you park and walk through a tunnel cut into the cliffs to the restaurant. It really is an amazing place and has the most spectacular view of any good local restaurant I have ever been to. It has local food and wine, which on a clear day with the cool mountain air and sparkling panoramic view will probably see you staying there for at least a couple of hours. From here, where the journey has taken you through the southern, dry side of the mountain range, you start to drop down the north side, which has more moisture, cooling winds, and therefore more vegetation and agriculture. You can either drive into Las Palmas and take the main coast road back, or cut through one of the other roads and shorten the trip, coming out near Playa del Ingles and Maspalomas. Near here is the area used for filming western-style cowboy films in Canon' Del Aguila.

The accommodation in Peurto Rico is almost entirely self-catering apartments which can either be booked through your local travel agent, or as I do, booked through a local woman, Mrs. Gay Oulton, who also organises the booking for the charter boats. You can contact her in writing: Mrs. Gay Oulton, c/o Insular S.A., Calle Alejandro Hidalgo 3, Las Palmas de Gran Canaria, Canary Islands. Some of the apartments are built way up on the valley walls and present a considerable walk back up if you leave something behind in the apartment. On the west wall of the valley overlooking the harbour and with their own restaurant are the Punta del Rey apartments. They are reached by some steps. On the floor level there are the Bahamas, Tobago and Caribe apartments all of which can be booked by Mrs. Oulton. Up in the extensive shopping plaza there are dozens of restaurants, bars and discos, which could best be described as the tourist area. There are no tackle shops so if you wish to try the shore fishing from the rocks and harbour outer wall you had better take your own. The charter boat price comes inclusive of any use of tackle, lures and bait.

The Fishing

Shore Fishing

Obviously the area directly around the harbour and beach is packed with tourists throughout the day, therefore it is best to confine any fishing to early morning or evening. The sport to be had directly in the harbour is strictly fun fishing. Although many years ago there were bluefish weighing in double figures to be caught, now there are only some mullet, and small European barracuda. The former are caught to only about 2 lbs in weight using a small spinning rod and very light line, probably not more than 3 lb breaking strain. Attract the mullet near you by using a mixture of sopped up bread and prawns, baiting with a tiny piece of

The commercial port of Arguineguin to the east of Peurto Rico has a thriving fishing industry. The prime quarry are skipjack tuna or bonito as they are known. Taken from these boats on bamboo poles, they can be sampled at the Bar Marino in the evening. July is not only the best month for marlin, but also the time of the local carnival, making an evening all the more colourful.

bread or prawn on a size 12 freshwater hook. You can either watch them take visually and strike, or if there is a wind putting a ripple on the water, you can use a small quill float. You can get them right around where the charter boats moor, but I have had better size fish from the square boulders near the mouth of the harbour. Here there is a slight flow of water, and you can drift out pieces of crust. Also inside the harbour, often lying in the shade of the boat hulls are small barracuda to about 2 lbs. I have seen them caught on tiny spinners on a flood tide late in the evening, and I think a small livebait would be quite good. Fishing from the outer harbour wall you can take mullet, plus a wide variety of tiny bream like reef fish that live in among the rock cracks and crevices. They barely grow larger than about a pound in weight, but as I said, this represents fun fishing, when you want to kill half a day.

By cutting one of the reef fish in half and casting it out as far as possible with a weight, then fishing at dusk it should be possible to take stingray from the shore. I have heard of this being tried with the occasional big fish being lost, and while it is always difficult to ascertain what species did the damage I am confident it will be the stingrays. Occasionally, just very occasionally, it will be worth distance casting with a heavy metal lure from any of the rocks for bluefish, but its best to ask the locals first if they are being caught by the inshore boats. Bluefish are gamefish, scrapping very hard, so it is common sense to see if they are within distance of the shore.

Boat Fishing

The boat fishing can be divided into three categories. Trolling, which means dragging lures along behind a moving boat. Drifting and chumming, by which you motor the game boat out to deep water, stop the engines and drift the ocean currents and winds, at the same time throwing over pieces of small fish to attract larger predators. Then anchoring, which can either be tying up to a deepwater buoy for tuna attracted by chumming, or anchoring closer in to shore on level sandy ground and fishing for big stingray. As the fuel outlay is minimal for the latter method, it is one most popular with the tourist. He wants to catch a fish quickly, and so this bottom fishing allows him the best chance, and at a reasonable price. From Peurto Rico there are about a dozen hire boats and a few private boats that fish these waters. Some that Mrs. Oulton can book are as follows. *Dorado* is a 34 foot catamaran hull gameboat that has fished these waters for years. It can be very successful. Another is *Felusi*, another cat, this time 35 feet long, and Jose the skipper is very good at finding a good stingray mark. The *Carmen* is a 38 foot gameboat built on the tradional Spanish design and run by a father and son team who are both called Francisco, which can lead to some problems during the day. They may possibly be the best boat for finding marlin and tuna offshore, their knowledge of the waters is second to none. Four other boats are fishing the waters regularly: *Alcor 3, Alcor 4, Spica* and *Barakuda*.

While Mrs. Oulton can give you most of the information you would require for a week or so fishing, more detailed information can be obtained from the International Game Fish Association representative, Mr. Chris Roncoroni. He can be contacted at The Tauro Country Club, Mogan, Gran Canaria.

For the angler wanting to go out for stingray it is best to point out that they have been landed to 200 lbs on rod and line. This is rare,

A massive haul of stingrays to 68 lbs and the bonus of a shark was landed by this group of British anglers on this expedition organised by the author. Left to right: Colin Shaw, Gary Dee, Chris Kent and Bob Burchett were all happy with their day's sport. Puerto Rico stingrays have been landed to several hundred pounds, so make sure you are fit.

but nevertheless a possibility. The average size would be nearer 30 or 40 lbs, still quite a creditable fish on light tackle. If you are inexperienced and don't want to risk losing your first fish, you should use the boat's 80 lb class tackle. This is more than ample for anything that comes along. If you want a bit more sport from the fish drop down to the 50 lb class, which can be used standing up with the additional aids of a butt pad and shoulder harness. In my opinion, perfectly adequate for the fish, you might even get a decent bend in an English 50 lb blank! This is the lightest category tackle you are likely to find aboard a charter boat, so anything lighter you will have to bring yourself. The experienced angler will want to use a 30 lb outfit which of course is living a little dangerously should anything too large come along. I recently used a Fenwick 20 lb class rod, and one of the new Shimano TLD 20's filled with 20 lb test Ande monofilament line, and by using a Sampo butt pad and harness managed to weigh in a stingray of 53 lbs! On 50 lb tackle the largest I have taken was a 94 lb butterfly ray, aboard the *Felusi*.

When you hook a stingray he immediately throws sand over his body and suctions himself to the bottom. A novice can therefore stay attached to even a moderate ray for up to twenty minutes before the pressure on the rod starts the fish moving and line can be gained. My tip is this. Once you detect a bite, allow some line to run off the spool unhindered, but taking care not to allow a backlash to develop. Then put the reel drag on maximum, wind out the stretch like a madman and strike and wind until you have the fish off the bottom. It is a way of suprising the stingray before he has time to realise he is hooked, and keeps him from suctioning on the bottom. The nearer the stingrays come to the surface the easier the fight gets. Their sting by the way is not located in the tip of the tail, but about halfway down. It is a long serrated spine sticking out, and although unlikely to kill, will be excruciatingly painful if embedded in a careless foot. Most of the rays are brought in for either food or weighing, but I see no reason to not release a few or all of your catch for another day. The skippers seem to think that if you return a ray it will stop the fishing altogether, but I find this difficult to believe, although I have also heard it said of other species. The bait used will generally be either a bunch of four sardines or baby mackerel hooked onto a 4 foot mono leader of 200 lbs or so. Wire leaders are not required. I have also taken them on pieces of tuna fillet.

To pass the time you can always drop down a set of baited small hooks to see what you can come up with. I have heard of big grouper being landed to forty pounds and also bream to twelve pounds. Generally it will be a mixture of goggle eyed reef fish, a proportion of which will be poisonous. Some of these can put you in hospital, and the weaver, which in England grows to a few ounces, can be over 6 lbs in the Canary Isles. Better by far to let the crew unhook the fish for you. While you are anchored you can also put a shark line down, and may possibly get a run from a shark of undetermined species to about 80 lbs in weight. The bigger pelagic sharks are found in deeper water near the dropoff to the continental shelf.

If the rays are not in an obliging mood you can ask the crew to try slow trolling with magnum Rapala lures close in to the coastline cliffs. Here you have an outside chance of a basking wahoo, a bluefish or a European barracuda, the latter a thin, poor fighting fish and not a patch on the bigger great barracuda more popular with anglers.

The method of chumming at anchor is simple, yet at the right time, devastatingly effective. The boat is tied up to a pre-anchored bouy, usually about five miles offshore. There can be a strong current here, and the crew will continually cut up small pieces of mackerel or sardine and drop them over the side to twinkle and flash in the clear blue water. The first fish to arrive are usually the Spanish mackerel. Built like our own mackerel they have blotchy markings rather than the crinkled striations of markings on their backs like the UK variety. The crew will put a couple or three live mackerel on each rod and drift one way on a balloon at a predetermined depth, the other two will fish freelined into the current. This method is very much a waiting game as it is too deep here to bottom fish, so you must keep a lookout on top and through the water for any signs of a big fish. You may catch any one of a number of different shark species. Blue, mako, hammerhead and thresher to several hundred pounds have all been landed. More likely you will be in search of a big tuna – yellowfin, bigeye or one of the huge bluefins that are known to migrate past this coast. They have been landed to over 900 lbs in weight, so be prepared for a fight of several hours. To be truthful the tuna fishing was fantastic in the late seventies but they then had a lean spell. These islands all have very deep water surrounding them so there is no form of shallow ground to hold the baitfish, and thereby the predators. Everything is on the move, migrating past, and it depends just how close to the coast they come. A mile in the wrong place and they swim straight past! Boats tend to troll for the blue marlin, white marlin and spearfish, but trolling fast with artifical lures is not the best way of contacting a big bluefin tuna. It is always worth trying for at least one day of a fishing holiday as part of the sport is the mystery of the unknown, and the adventure of the pursuit.

Drifting and chumming is the same principle for attracting either tuna or shark, but it is done from a moving boat. So rather than using the attraction of the small fish in the chum to bring the predators to you, the gameboat is constantly on the move and will hopefully find the fish and hold them with the attraction of its titbits of free offerings. This method is usually followed when the ocean current is so strong that the pre-moored buoys have been pulled under by the water pressure, and the skipper is unable to anchor. Also with a stronger current the boat will be covering more area.

The final way of offshore fishing is by trolling. This entails pulling artificial lures behind the boat, in an effort to make them seem like fleeing baitfish. Now most of the boats will be going after marlin, but if you are a novice and just want to catch a fish, you could do worse than rig up with 20 lb class tackle and put on a small plastic squid about three inches long, with a 1/4 ounce of lead in its plastic head. This is taken on the troll by skipjack tuna, which run about five pounds each, but despite their small size are game fighters on light tackle, and providing they can be located in a school, can be hooked several at a time. You may even wish to try the local method of fishing them commercially using a heavy 16 foot bamboo pole, skipping the lure over the waves and swinging the fish up in one easy movement. It's not as easy as it sounds as the fish must be kept head up the split second he takes the lure. This means immense pressure initially and could be a painful mistake if you fail to hold the pole in the correct position. I pride myself that on a boat full of experienced fishermen recently I was the only one to extract a tuna successfully using this pole method!

The marlin are caught, or should I say fished for, by the same method of trolling as used for the skipjacks (called locally bonito), but big artificial lures are used. It is a technique that I specialise in myself and have taken blue marlin to over 500 lbs using it, and have hooked as many as seven marlin in one day. The artificial lures are made mostly in America, where I have found the following to be the best and most productive makes on

The author with a 220 lb marlin he landed from Peurto Rico, on a Murray Brothers' marlin lure. The fish was beaten in 20 minutes.

the market: Murray Brothers 'Lite N' Glow', Sevenstrand Clones, Softheads, Lurco, and Sir-Ace. These are trolled at speeds up to eight knots the whole day, changing their position behind the boat as conditions allow. On a rough day they may have to be fished a long way back, on a calm day, closer to the stern. It all depends on making the right action thus simulating a frantically fleeing baitfish. It is essential that the lure pops up to the surface, collects a pocket of air then dives down, leaving a trail of air bubbles rippling behind its plastic skirt. Usually only four marlin lures will be fished but by careful presentation using double-tag lines and AFTCO roller troller outrigger clips I have successfully run eight lures. If a marlin strike occurs you must help assist in winding the other lures out of the way, and the angler whose fish it is, gets into the fighting chair and is harnessed up to the reel. At no time is he strapped to the fighting chair, only the reel and rod, which is capable of dragging him overboard if the reel seizes up. The crewmate will tell you how much pressure to apply to the drag, but for marlin strikes the setting is usually quite substantial, so be prepared for quite a bit of pressure when the reel is harnessed up. The fight can last anything from ten minutes to four hours, depending on how big the fish is, whether he fights deep or shallow, and how inexperienced the angler is. The average Canary Isles blue marlin would probably run about 250 lbs, although fish to over 700 lbs are taken each season. Smaller lures

All action as a rare longbill spearfish is brought aboard for captor Jerry Airey from Essex. As many as four marlin have been caught from one boat in one day, but this is very much a rarity. The spearfish weighed over 60 lbs.

and much lighter tackle are advised for those wishing to get more sport from their fish.

The smaller white marlin are almost a by-product of anglers out after the blue, and run only 40 to 80 lbs in weight, although Peurto Rico has recorded them to just over 100 lbs. Another species is the longbill spearfish, often mistaken, for the white marlin, it is long and slim and best fished for with light tackle. The trouble is they are so rare, that the moment you put out some light 20 lb tackle for a spearfish, a small blue marlin comes along! These run to 40 to 70 lbs, and are a rarity value rather than a sporting proposition. The charter boats will want you to fish with the maximum tackle class of 130 lb breaking strain line, and if you have never caught a blue marlin before it is really the best way to go. Yet if you are experienced and have taken a few before, then 80 lb class is far more fun, and 50 lb class literally exciting. To give you some idea of how good the marlin run can be it is first best to realise that the migration can go through virtually anytime from June to October. In one mad week of fishing the charter fleet landed a staggering *sixteen* blue marlin, one the largest ever at 902 lb. Francisco Ortega, the owner and skipper of the gameboat *Carmen* took the record catch with three blue marlin caught in one day. To Europe's amazement he took the *Carmen* out the next day and broke his own record by landing FOUR blue marlin in one day, a record that is still standing and very unlikely to get beaten. The depths about five miles offshore run to 1200 feet, which is the first of the dropoffs that cause the upwelling of plankton, bait and predators. The biggest ever marlin to be landed commercially weighed 1375 lbs and every year a fish approaching or in excess of 1000 lbs is landed commercially. Most are taken by handliners who catch a bonito which is in turn taken by the monster marlin.

As for the size of the bluefin tuna: in their heyday of 1979 the *Dorado* gameboat took nine bluefin tuna for a total combined weight of 5073 lbs in just ten days' fishing. That historic year of 1979 saw more than a hundred of these giant bluefin tuna brought to gaff, showing just how fantastic the fishing can be when these leviathans decide to migrate past the coastline within reach of the charter fleet. The average weight of the bluefin tuna that year was 550 lbs.

Of the known records of different species taken by the Canarian commercial fisherman, these are the outstanding fish: dolphin (fish) 70 lbs, albacore 92½ lbs, bluefin tuna 1250 lbs, broadbill swordfish 691 lbs, and Atlantic blue marlin an amazing

1657 lbs, way above the world record for a rod and line caught fish. At one point this small island of Gran Canaria held no less than 22 world records for tuna in the various line classes presided over by the International Game Fish Association in Florida, USA. The rod and line records for the island are as follows: yellowfin 286 lbs, bigeye tuna 363 lbs, and skipjack tuna 21 lbs. A white marlin weighing a massive 143 1/4 lbs was landed back in 1977, so you can visualise the standards these waters are capable of setting. But the fishing is far from easy. You are either lucky or not in the timing of your trip, as fish that run through one week in July will not run the same time the following year. You can book up a year in advance and you may still book the wrong time. The fish, unfortunately, don't know what time you are going on holiday! As a basic guide you could expect tuna in April and May, mainly bigeye. Some white marlin in May. Blue marlin from June to October, although April 1987 saw a 770 pounder caught, which is exceedingly early. The main run for blues would be the last three weeks in July and the first in August. Wahoo have been taken in numbers in rough waters where the wind skirts the island to the east in the month of October. Sharks and stingrays can be expected year round, and bonito from April to October.

Although these 'Fortunate Isles' have Gran Canaria as the main staging post for their big game boats, it is worth noting that as soon as some enterprising soul starts a boat operating from any of the other islands, that you should take my advice and try it. Fish have fins, and these ocean wanderers don't just confine themselves to Gran Canaria!

GREECE

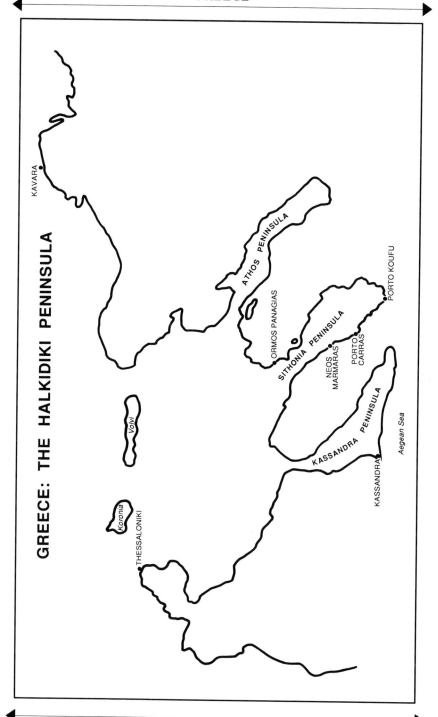

GREECE: THE HALKIDIKI PENINSULA

KAVARA

ATHOS PENINSULA

ORMOS PANAGIAS

PORTO KOUFU

SITHONIA PENINSULA

NEOS MARMARAS

PORTO CARRAS

Volvi

KASSANDRA PENINSULA

Aegean Sea

Koronia

KASSANDRA

THESSALONIKI

While a great many anglers will think of much of the Mediterranean as a polluted fishless void, it may come as something as a surprise to learn that the waters off Greece may just have good fishing. The Mediterranean has little in the way of tidal flow, the tideline moving only a few feet in most places. For this reason it was believed that the pollutants which many countries pump, and continue to pump into the ocean, were staying there, building up over a period of time, and therefore keeping any fish away. I make no pretence at suggesting the waters of the Med are as clean and pure as the open Atlantic (even that great volume of ocean is not without its pollution). What I am saying is that there are still many fish in certain parts of the Mediterranean Sea, certainly enough to warrant an exploratory trip or two while on holiday. That the huge bluefin tuna run these waters has been known for centuries, but on a recent trip up to Greece, I found that they, along with several other species of gamefish, were patrolling the area of the North Aegean Sea. Obviously this is an item of interest to many people as Greece and its splendid islands have long been a favourite venue for the package tour operators. The immaculate blue skies, burning temperatures and clear beaches have attracted the British holidaymaker for over twenty years. With the advent of more islands being made available to the holiday market, obviously the number of brochures and travel magazines have blossomed, thereby offering holidays to every corner of Greece and its islands. Access could never be simpler, all you have to do is walk into your nearest travel agent and ask to see the travel brochures for Greece. There are many, but as the area I have caught fish from is fairly explicit, I will deal only with that area. I have no doubt that these same fish can be caught from dozens of as yet undiscovered places, possibly the very same islands that are so popular with the British holidaymaker. Yet again, like so many countries, the potential is there for a charter fishing facility, but nobody has taken the plunge and started it.

Travel Tips

Access

There are scheduled flights direct from Heathrow to Thessalonika, which is on the Halkidiki peninsula. These run on a Saturday or Wednesday, although you can also fly via British Caledonian to Amsterdam from Gatwick and then with Olympic to Thessalonika. Of course that is the way to go if you just need a flight out there and already have somewhere to stay or are met by friends. A cheaper way is by buying a charter flight seat from the main tour operators like Thomsons, Intasun or Wings. Again, that is a flight only, so you will need a contact or friend when you get there. If it is your first time to Greece, and I would venture this suggestion for any first time visit to a new country, take one of the all-in package deals. This is by far the most reasonable mode of travel, featuring accommodation and travel, also food as included in the price. You may be tied as such to a particular hotel, but you are not tied to set activities. Intasun for instance can fly you on one of their package holidays, from Gatwick to Thessalonika airport, with a flying time of just 3 hours 35 minutes. Generally the flights are scheduled to be operated by Air Europe Airtours, Dan Air, Monarch Airlines, British Island Airways and Paramount Airways using Boeing 757,737,727, Airbus, Tristar and BAC 1-11 aircraft. You need to check in up to 1¹/2 hours prior to departure time, and the baggage allowance may be restricted to 15kg. Again, if you have reels or heavier items of fishing tackle, take them with you in your hand baggage. You may also find it beneficial to notify the carriers beforehand that you intend taking fishing rods, and give them dimensions of your rod carrying tube. Charter flights are often heavily booked and they need to know the shape and size of anything other than a regular suitcase.

Health & Immigration

There are no special stipulations regarding entry into Greece, and you need just a valid British passport. Also a British Visitor's passport is valid, but children under 16 years of age who are

The bustling tiny harbour of Porto Koufu, near the tip of the Sithonia peninsula, indicates there are plenty of fish to be caught. If you visit here, try a salad and local wine from a small café near the water.

included on an adult's passport may not travel unless accompanied by that adult. A point worth noting is that any visitors with a passport stamp showing entry into Turkey or North Cyprus may be refused entry. Also if you visit Greece on a charter flight, you will not be able to visit any other country during the trip. Remember that if you are applying for a British passport to allow at least eight weeks to obtain or renew it. There are no compulsory health vaccinations required, but it is advisable to consult with your local G.P. in case he personally advises one. It pays to take along your own mini-pack of First Aid comprising plasters, bandage, paracetamol (or similar), Diocalm, cough mixture, indigestion tablets etc. There will be pharmacists at most places, and many of the larger hotels have their own room and house doctor, but these small items often provide a remedy without recourse to expensive doctors. It is also advisable to ensure that the medical section of your travel insurance provides sufficient cover.

Ground Transportation

There are usually plenty of taxis around, but these are generally quite expensive. The local buses are better, and you can check at the reception desk of your hotel which villages they visit, and what the approximate timings are. If you are arriving on a package holiday all ground transportation from the airport will be taken care of. Generally you are met by the relevant tour representative, who will escort you to your waiting coach, which then whisks you to the appropriate hotel. If you intend hiring a car and 'doing your own thing' in Greece, you will need a valid British driver's licence. Again, your tour rep can assist you with any booking, but take note that it can become very expensive. They have a mileage rate that is high, and the cost of fuel and insurance is also high. If I remember correctly a car I hired and toured the peninsula with, clocking up over 200 miles, set four of us back just under £60. We saw a lot of the country, but it had worked out a lot more than taking an organised excursion!

Accommodation

There are two types of popular accommodation used by the package tour operators. The hotel, which includes every facility you might require. Or the self-catering apartment or villa which allows you unrestricted freedom to buy food at the local supermarket and sample some of the local recipes. If it is your first trip to Greece I suggest the hotel, where you are looked after by a tour rep and have access to the organised tours. If your second trip, try a villa or apartment, which I confess to liking more myself, as fishing does not conform to the timing of hotel meals. With the self-catering aspect you do really need a hire car, but the rate for an extended period of a week or more should see a drop in the rental price. Failing that, a cheap way to get about from apartments is by mopeds or motorbike, but take note that the standards of maintenance in Greece are something less than you would find in the UK. If you get a good one, that's fine, but Intasun actually strongly advise against their hiring, not only because maintenance is dubious, but because the road surfaces are of an inferior standard to the UK.

The hotels are situated on the Halkidiki peninsula in the

north-east corner of the Aegean Sea, and the place I fished from was a new complex at Porto Carras. The nearby village of Neos Marmaras is where Intasun have their apartments, and if you like self-catering, this little fishing village is the ideal place to stay. The Pegasus Studios and Apartments are run by a gentleman with an English wife, which of course as far as language barriers go is an advantage in itself. Set back with a view, the apartments are about 400 yards from the nearest tavernas and supermarkets. Just a few yards from the rocky edge of the water, there is a small shingle cove about 150 yards away and a sandy beach over on the other side of the village. The Alexandra Studios are located in a quiet residential part of Neos Marmaras and are half a mile from the village centre. The Kilo Studios are ideal for two to three people, about 150 yards from the nearest shops, but a word of warning, they are up a steep walk. You can also take the taxi boat that leaves from the jetty in the harbour down to Porto Carras. The Eleni rooms are apartments that have only recently been built, and are set right in the centre of the town with supermarkets and so on all on the doorstep. The final apartments in this area that will interest fishermen are the Yiannis Rooms. These are also in a new building some 450 yards down a side street, from the centre of the town. There are regular buses to Thessalonika, and of course all the other local amenities in nearby Porto Carras.

Porto Carras is a new holiday resort complex complete with all sports facilities and a modern fitted marina. There is an 18-hole golf course, tennis courts, riding stables and swimming pool. It was built by a John Carras, a Greek shipping magnate of incredible wealth who had a vast concept that has been turned into reality. Three luxury hotels were planned, two are finished, the other is not, but the hotels, together with their own village, can house 5000 people. 230 million dollars later, there was a change of government which left the project about 60% completed. However that remaining 60% is still operable and it is from here that the fishing boat leaves. The holiday season in this part of Greece runs approximately from April to November, but a smaller hotel was built near the marina in an effort to generate year-round tourism. By taking a package holiday you not only stay during the months governed by the brochures, but you stay at the best time of fishing as well. Porto Carras is about 120km from the airport, and located well down the Sithonia peninsula, the centre finger of three pieces of land that project down into the Aegean Sea. The two hotels are called the Sithonia Beach and the Meliton Beach, both having restaurants that offer a wide spectrum of cuisine. The grounds are just part of a massive 4500 acres of countryside, and stretch along more than 10km of secluded coves and sandy beaches. The estate is surrounded by rolling hills, which are covered with the lush greenery of a million vines, and colourful groves of almond and citrus trees.

Take a continental multiadaptor for the electricity if you have a hair dryer or electric shaver. For currency I recommend you take sterling travellers' cheques and change them either at the hotel bank, or a bank at the airport. All banks take a commission, but at least if you have travellers' cheques you have some form of insurance if they are lost or stolen. It is said you can drink the water, but I always try to get hold of some bottles of mineral water, both to keep in the bedrooms for drinking, and for things like washing your teeth, or washing cuts etc. I see no point in risking things, when for a nominal sum you can buy safety in the shape of a plastic bottle of water. You can shop quite late in the hotels, and in the nearby village of Neos Marmaras. In fact it seems they stay open, as long as there are tourists walking around.

The Area

The three peninsulas of the mainland project from Thessalonika as three fingers, into the Aegean Sea. The western tip of land is the Kassandra peninsula, the centre is Sithonia, and the third is Athos. For this reason you get the feeling that you are on a Greek island, especially on the Kassandra peninsula, with its magnificent long sandy beaches. As a backdrop you have silvery olive groves and dark pinewoods scattering the hillsides. Sithonia has many fishing villages and coves, making a tour of the local tavernas and bars a pleasure. Most easterly of the three is Mount Athos, where as many as a hundred monasteries cluster its magnificent steep sides, and where women have been totally banned. The peak of the mountain itself rises 6200 feet straight out of the sea, and can be photographed on a tour by boat. From the north-east corner of Sithonia, at Ormos Panagias, a steamer tours right down the coast to let you take photographs of this historic area, and to see the splendour of the monasteries, some almost built onto the edge of the mountain.

The Fishing

Shore Fishing

I would classify the shore fishing in this area as being poor. There is no point in beating about the bush, there are two species worth trying for and they are the mullet that frequent the marina at Porto Carras and the harbour at Neos Marmaras, and the carp that live in the ornamental lakes in the middle of the golf course. I shall

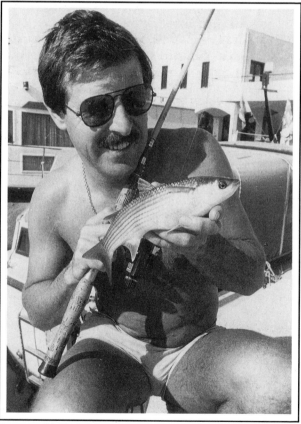

No monster fish this time, but the marina at Porto Carras has shoals of mullet that require a little more skill in capture than the tuna shoals of deep water. Let those of you cynical about the mullet's size, try to catch 30 lbs of them in a morning!

deal with the latter first, as the tackle used for both species can be the same. I heard about these two lakes on the golf course at the back of the hotel from somebody at the riding stables. I took a recce with a fishing rod one evening when the course was closing. The two lakes were very green with algae, and I hurriedly crossed the fairway to a single bush that was planted on the bank edge. In front of me I thought I saw some pieces of wood bobbing around in clumps. It was in fact groups of carp. With shaking hands, I cast out my float, hook baited with a double helping of bread and hope... and waited! The wait took about seven seconds and I was attached to a 5 lb carp that went careering off around pool. After six carp in successive casts, I beat a hasty retreat to the hotel room, blurting out my discovery to my wife, who remained, as usual, impassive. Next morning a friend and I risked frontal lobotomy from a golf ball as we hammered carp after carp from that pool. After we had taken a staggering 123 lbs of carp, the inevitable happened. A jeep rolled up, and out jumped the greenkeeper with arms gesticulating wildly. I speak no Greek but could tell he wasn't in the least amused. We pleaded temporary insanity and he ordered us off. The fishing was nothing short of stupendous, but obviously out of bounds (although if a person was to get up at 5am and fish until 7am, they might miss the greenkeeper?). My final tip on this is to use your 'loaf'. Enough said!

The mullet are to be found right underneath the restaurant window of the Meliton hotel, which is hardly surprising, as the guests have a habit of throwing their rolls into the water saying, 'OOh, look at the fish'. These mullet have, I am sure you have already guessed, a definite bent towards bread. Should that bread be a tiny piece of flake pinched onto a size 18 freshwater hook, 1 lb line and 2 bb float, then you will catch them. The reason for this frailness of tackle is due to the fact that a few of the locals know about the mullet as well. The difference is that they throw out a handline of 20 lb monofilament at the end of which is a whole roll. Underneath this floating roll there are up to six sets of treble hooks! The mullet cluster round the roll to nibble at the crust and when enough have congregated...WHAM! a hard jerk on the line rips a hook into a fish. As far as I can see from this dubious method there appears to be a jerk on both ends of the line! These mullet move right up in between the moored boats, especially during the hours of early morning and late evening. However it can be said that they have no fear of boats moving about in the marina, rather than spooking completely they simply move out of casting range until the boat has gone. Then by the introduction of some extra feed they can be lured back into casting range and caught again. The locals eat these mullet, but there's no reason why a sportsfisherman shouldn't put them back for another person to catch. If the Aegean Sea were stacked with toothy predators like wahoo and kingfish I would readily keep them and rig them up as bait. But there are no predators other than the tuna, so if you must keep them for a photograph why not use a freshwater keep net to retain them, then return them alive?

As far as my own expeditions along the rocks are concerned, the mullet are virtually the only fish worth catching from the shore. The water seems clear enough, but I came up with absolutely nothing when I tried an evening/night session using a big piece of bait on the bottom. Although many hotel beaches are covered in people thrashing around in the sea during daytime, the fish often move right in amongst the swimmers. Many is the time I have snorkelled along a crowded beach and seen mullet, snappers and various species of bream in amongst the swimmers. In Mauritius in the Indian Ocean you can actually attract small fish up to a couple of pounds by standing in four feet of water and swirling up the coarse coral sand at your feet. It must release tiny organisms on which these fish feed, and this beach area in front of the two hotels might be the same. Perhaps a couple of nights prebaiting with a bread and fish mix may bring them in to feed, but I still have the feeling it will only be the odd bream or snapper that shows. Presumably they must have big stingrays, but I never saw any on the commercial boats, and I certainly never hooked any. My advice would be to stick to the mullet in the harbour, and if you get the chance, that wonderful carp fishing.

Boat Fishing

When I visited Porto Carras, it was to meet the man who told me about the fishing. Mr. Takis Tragakis was someone I met on a trip I had touring South Africa, and while in Cape Town I stopped at his house. We were to spend half a day fishing for a great white, but that, as they say, is another story. Takis was talking all the time about the super tuna fishing off Porto Carras, and how excited he was to have discovered several species that could be taken, and which were classed as international gamefish. I was as sceptical as the next fisherman when it came to believing any story about fish in the Med, let alone gamefish, but Takis had the pictures to prove it, so on my return from Cape Town, I set up a trip that would allow me to see some of this new fishing potential. It was the same old story. The local people had no idea what a rod and reel was, and even the local commercial fishing fleet based farther south on the Sithonia peninsula at Porto Koufu, were still catching the tuna on long lines. Takis took his own boat there, and started trolling with South African squid lures. Almost immediately he started to catch longfin tuna, or albacore as they are known to anglers. This was the mainstay of the commercial fishermen, and they could not believe this method was even possible, let alone successful. Eventually he was told by his friends that the local fishermen

Here is the evidence that monster bluefin tuna also migrate through these waters. This 350 lb bluefin was photographed by the author from Porto Koufu, and had only been taken a short distance from where he was albacore fishing with rod and line.

didn't believe the albacore were taken trolling with pieces of plastic in the water, and that he was stealing their fish from the long lines and claiming they were caught on rod and line. Takis decided the only way to convince them was to take them out, which he did, and of course they caught the albacore, and some yellowfin tuna on rod, reel and plastic lure. Having alleviated any fear the commercials had, he searched around to find the best areas, times of day, month and lure until one day he returned to port with a massive haul of over 45 albacore and yellowfin tuna. He tried again and took over 30 tuna, finding out that a wind blowing from the north-east quarter put the tuna down. Anything with a rough sea lowered the catch rate, while, as soon as it flattened off, the tuna rose to the surface, generally in late afternoon, and struck the lures well. Besides having albacore and yellowfin tuna off the tip of the Sithonia peninsula, he found that immense bluefin tuna roamed the water.

I was standing on the beach one evening when I saw a flock of seabirds diving not half a mile distant. As a specialist fisherman myself, I knew that underneath the birds were feeding fish, but the boils on the top of the water seemed enormous. I told Takis, and he informed me they were giant bluefin tuna. Next morning we trolled the area, and I actually saw a couple of big swirls on the surface, but these tuna were unlikely to take a lure. Takis had been spooled out completely on 80 lb line a few times, knowing they were the bluefin, and knowing that the fish were mostly in excess of 1000 lbs. These giants feed close into shore, possibly chasing a shoal of sardines along the coast, and they could just take a livebait trolled slowly along just underneath the surface. One I saw up on the docks at Porto Koufu had been taken by a commercial longliner fishing for albacore. It weighed, I would estimate around 350 lbs. Takis assures me that they had been landed to 3000 lbs.

The sardine fishermen also knew of another prized gamefish that swam in these waters. They saw the broadbill swordfish at night in the area of water lit by the arc lamps of their caiques (boats) as they fished for the sardine. At Porto Koufu I saw a prepared carcass of a swordfish, which looked as if it weighed about a hundred pounds. These could possibly be taken if you could go out at night with one of these commercials and fish on rod and line with either squid or sardine onto which is tied a red or green Cyalume chemical lightstick. This is an accepted method in America, and probably never before tried in Greece. Further investigation revealed that marlin also run these waters, and that even the dolphin (fish, not mammal) are caught. I have a photo of a fish caught in a Greek competition from Porto Carras and it is certainly one of the billfish family, probably a white marlin. They also have various species of sharks that feed on the sardine shoals and some spearfish. The tuna are reported to be in their thickest numbers around mid September to November, although Takis has taken them at the end of July and the beginning of August. The fishing hotspot is from the tip of Kassandra peninsula across to Sithonia peninsula then over again to Mount Athos. This puts you in a dropoff area of 200 metres to 1000 metres, an ideal area for baitfish, where any currents converge. The moon appears to have no effect on the tuna fishing, whereas in almost every other country in the world it has a marked bearing on them. Barometric pressure and wind direction can put them down, and it is these that Takis puts most interest in. He often fishes the same area as the commercials, who lay up to five 5 kilometre longlines, each with 600 hooks about 3/0 in size. Bait is invariably a sardine and the depths are quite shallow at 4 metres. Trolling around a commercial as he is working is a very successful way of taking all species of tuna, especially the albacore.

Takis first started this pioneering fishing with rod and line way back in 1976, using his own boat the *Anna Katarina*, a 42 foot Chris Craft that was about fourteen years old. It has a range of 400 miles, and he purchased it in Nice, France where it had only been used as a gin-palace. It is fitted with twin GM 260 hp engines, plus all the latest in electronic radios, direction seekers and sounders to ensure he knows exactly where he is. The boat is fitted with the same type of rod holders as I found in South Africa, whereby the rods are in a horizontal position for trolling instead of vertical, and thereby the strike is taken straight on the reel, rather than the rod. Using outriggers, adjustable vertical rod holders, and these flat-line rod holders, Takis is able to run up to nine rods at once, often resulting in multiple hookups of several fish. The action the lures put into the water behind the boat must look like a shoal of sardines fleeing to them. When I fished with Takis it was the end of September, and I must point out that while the fishing was good, it was virtually the last week in the tourist season and everywhere in the hotel was closing down. If you decide to go to catch the best run of albacore and yellowfins I would advise booking an apartment to enable you to 'do your own thing'. That way you won't get the impression that all the hotel staff are waiting to close down! The size of the fish are not particularly high on average when we went fishing. I suppose the albacore were averaging about 8 lbs each, although we took them up to 16 lbs, and the yellowfins slightly larger. They possibly average 15 lbs apiece and run to nearly 50 lbs. These are all school fish, so find one and you are likely to hook others. The giant bluefins are liable to remain uncaught as running over 8 lines on a boat is asking for trouble. These big fish have the power of a runaway train, even on

Here is the proof that the North Aegean Sea plays host to some vast shoals of tuna, including albacore, yellowfin and bluefin. The author (centre) was delighted with this 18-fish albacore catch with individual fish to 16 lbs in weight. All were taken on rod and line using plastic lures trolled in the deep water off the Sithonia Peninsula. English angler Chris Kent (left) was on his first ever gamefishing trip, and (right) the man who discovered the fish, Mr. Takis Tragakis.

130 lb test tackle, so all the time you are trying to clear the other lines away the one with the fish attached will either break from the speed of the take, or have the line emptied from the reel. To give you some sort of idea of the power involved in this species, a specimen hooked on heavy 80 lb tackle by Takis was stripped completely before it broke away. The length of time it took to happen?... just 45 seconds on Takis' estimation! Another he fought on rod and reel for a longer period. This one he stayed attached to for 9½ hours before it broke the line only a few yards from the boat. At Metilini on the mainland these big tuna are harpooned after being attracted to the boat when it was chumming, or groundbaiting with chunks of fish. They have had them weighed to 1250kg, and estimated to 1900kg. Some of these fish are also reputed to have had a long, thin plastic tag attached. Obviously worth nothing they were discarded, but they could show an important migratory pattern on a global scale, as fish already tagged by anglers off the north-east seaboard of the United States have shown long migratory patterns. The flesh of the bluefin tuna is highly prized when served as a raw delicacy in Japan, and commands a fantastic price, so this may be the reason these tagged fish are kept quiet. With such good money to make fishing commercial for them, it is common sense that the fishermen would not wish to reveal the tuna's whereabouts!

Takis is currently moving his boat from place to place in an effort to establish a proper sportfishing centre, and was last heard of with his mother on the island of Lesbos. Porto Carras would have been the ideal situation for a sportfishing centre with good, cheap package holidays, admirable weather conditions and relatively easy access. The marina together with all its facilities were there, and the big engines on the *Anna Katarina* pushed her quickly out to where the deep water at the end of the peninsulas began. It is a great place for a holiday with some shore fishing thrown in anyway, but it would also be good to get a day or two out after the tuna. There may by now be more boats chartering from Porto Carras, so check with your package company first. The other possibility is to write to the National Tourist Organisation of Greece, 195/197 Regent Street, London WIR 8DL, tel: 01-734-5997 and see if they have any contact for the whereabouts of Takis Tragakis. You could also enquire of his whereabouts to the General Manager of the Sithonia and Meliton Hotels, via your travel agent.

THE
GAMBIA

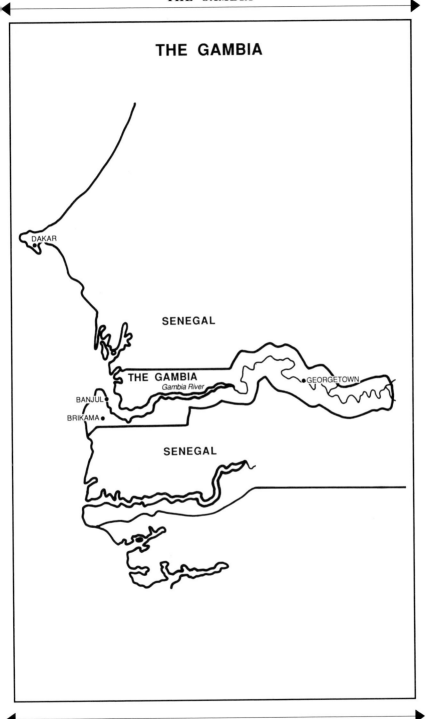

Travel Tips

Although it may well seem strange to include an African country in a book for European fishermen, you only have to look at the Canary Islands to realise just how close they are to the coast of Africa, and the Gambia is only a little further on. Also some of the leading package tour operators go there so it is still within the realms of reasonable prices.

Africa as a whole is, obviously, vast and the lack of development in many of its countries, means that probably over 90% or more of its fish-rich waters have never seen a rod and line. There are no gamefish of any numbers on the north coast of the continent, the east coast has good fishing for sailfish, shark and marlin, and the south coast has an abundance of virtually everything that swims. West Africa also has most of the gamefish around its shores, and Dakar, in nearby Senegal, has turned into a leading area for the marlin and sailfish enthusiast. The country of Gambia is a sliver of land spliced into Senegal and thereby should have the same fishing potential, yet it is so underdeveloped it may be a decade before somebody ventures offshore.

Access

There is no scheduled airline running a regular service in to The Gambia, so you are totally reliant on the availability of package tours. When I first went to the country it was on such a package tour, and I confess that although I experienced the 'cattle syndrome', the holiday really was enjoyable and would be ideal for those people wishing to take their first sample of Africa as a holiday venue. The main airlines chartering in there are Brittania and British Caledonian. Of the tour operators going there, one of the best is Thomson. They are probably Britain's number one holiday company and they state they offer the best quality holidays at unbelievably low prices. Flights into The Gambia go to Banjul airport, the six hour flight passing quite quickly and comfortably, usually aboard a Boeing 767 aircraft. Baggage allowance on some of these package tours may be down to 15kg (33 lbs) per person, instead of the usual 20kg (44 lbs). Better cut down your tackle to the bare essentials, and take reels and leads with you either in a coat with big pockets or in your hand baggage. Generally the CAA regulations now only allow one piece of hand baggage into the cabin, so make use of anything with large coat pockets. Check-in time at the UK port of embarkation is about 1 1/2 hours before take-off, but do allow time for bad weather. I say this because Gambia holidays are usually at their peak from November to March, when people want to get away from our freezing clime. That makes a rush drive to the airport in our winter a hazardous operation, so why not allow a bit longer for such eventualities as punctures? Departures from the UK go from Gatwick airport on a Wednesday, running from 21st October to 20th April. Take-off time is 09.45, which means you land at 22.15 in the evening.

Health & Immigration

It is always sensible to have innoculations against typhoid, cholera and polio when visiting anywhere on the North African continent. While a British visitor's passport is sufficient for most holidays (valid for one year), The Gambia requires a full five or ten year valid passport. Do allow sufficient time for the processing of your passport application before actually booking a holiday, as at times it can take as long as three months to process. No visas are required, but you will need to be in possession of a valid cholera and yellow fever vaccination certificate. Check with your local G.P. where you go for this, and don't be surprised if your arm aches for a day after the jab. It's only a dull ache, nothing painful. Although not required by law, you could do worse than to take some malaria tablets, obtainable from most leading chemists (you generally have to start a course about a week or so before you leave, and continue taking them a couple of weeks after you get back).

Also, take any first aid kit or medication you think you might need. Plasters, headache pills like paracetamol or similar, a bandage, cough mixture, Medinite, lozenges and some antiseptic cream. That way you can treat any minor cuts and scratches yourself. Don't wash any open cuts under the tap water – use bottled mineral water. Then apply some antiseptic cream and put on a plaster. While you should already have a realistic medical insurance, it saves a visit to the doctor or hospital, which may initially be expensive. Take also some Diocalm or similar remedy for upset stomach, as a fact of life is that this happens to more people in North Africa than in the UK. As for currency, it is often best to take sterling traveller's cheques with you and get them changed in the hotel or local bank. Although the rate will be higher, it is illegal to change money on the black market. Most of the tours will be fully escorted/guided so there is no need to take a driver's licence for car hire.

Ground Transportation

As soon as you clear customs control at Banjul airport you will be pounced upon by porters to carry your bags. It's entirely up to you, but they only take it a few yards outside to the tour bus, and invariably want money for it. It's the same the world over, so if you have plenty of cash to spray around you will undoubtedly receive the attentions of a vast number of porters! The tour operator should have a courier waiting to direct you to the coach, from where you will be despatched to your hotel. Other than this, all other transportation will be either on a guided tour, or by the local taxi. Make sure you haggle a bit over the taxi price, and if you get dropped off somewhere, don't pay him for the return trip until you actually want to return. You may never see him again!

Accommodation

Thomson run about five hotel holidays in this country, and they all seem pretty fair when I visited them. The city centre is Banjul and the closest hotel to this is the Hotel Atlantic. Situated on the outskirts and less than three quarters of a mile from the centre, it is right on the open beach and the massive Atlantic Ocean. You would be hard pushed to get much closer to the sea. Quite a few British people stay here and it has a high standard of comfort with a large pool, and a programme of exploring on tours for those who can't bring themselves to lie on the beach. The weather is superb, and most people can't get enough sun for the first day, especially if they've come from a lovely freezing, drizzly January in Britain. They have international cabaret, African dancing and folklore, fashion shows, and dancing in the evening. You can fish from the beach right in front of the hotel, but you will be surprised at how cold the water is. I swam only once while there, and found it better swimming in the hotel pools. They offer windsurfing and sailing as well as volleyball, beach games, squash and tennis.

Next down the line from Banjul is the Wadner Beach. This was scheduled to open again after refurbishment in October 1987, and is a complex of small buildings set in tropical gardens. Not the high-rise style of hotel, but leaning more towards the true African style, which I find more enjoyable. Two and half miles from the city, this hotel is also situated right on the beach, giving both sea and pool for those who swim. There are sun terraces, a tropical garden, and a coffee shop. In the evening there is a disco and live entertainment. The African dancers, were the best I had seen anywhere in Africa. There are security guards at the entrance to both ends of the hotel, as there are at most of the Gambian hotels, and beware of long walks down the beach on your own. Even while I was there two people were mugged. One had his glasses ripped off his face in broad daylight while walking the beach with his wife. Another two couples were held up in an alley in Banjul late at night, and robbed. Quite what they were doing there is beyond me, and you should excercise greater care than normal when walking in ones and twos. Better to go in a group for safety, or enlist the care of a security officer for a small fee. The Wadner Beach is ideally situated for those shore fishermen who want to try the sport down at Denton Bridge, where the action can be quite good, and is only a short taxi ride away. The taxis can be picked up just outside the security gate.

Moving along the coast a bit further you have the Sunwing Hotel. Set on a headland among tropical vegetation, it is some 7 1/2 miles from Banjul. The hotel is run by the Scandinavian Vingressor chain so the food is rated very highly by British holidaymakers who have stayed there. Large cold and hot dishes predominate the meals, and a large buffet breakfast is served. Most of the hotels say no food is to be taken out of the breakfast room, but almost everyone I know has managed to take enough out to make do for additional lunch on the beach. I'm not advising you take food out, you understand, just that others have done it, and I presume it to be a standard part of hotel fiddlededee. After dinner in the evenings there is dancing to a band, although this may be changed depending on what sort of entertainment is scheduled. The pool is set in an attractive sun terrace with a pool bar and ornamental gardens, plus there is an à la carte restaurant.

The Hotel Fajara is eleven miles from Banjul and is a friendly hotel with a range of facilities. There is an 18 hole, par 67 golf course on sand, a shop, hairdresser, pool, gardens leading to the beach, and a bar lounge. There are tennis courts nearby, crazy golf, volleyball and swimming. It has 93 main hotel bedrooms and 173 bungalows. Finally, the last hotel, and again built right on the ocean front is the Hotel Kombo beach. This is a stylish hotel with fine facilities, and the beautiful Kotu beach right outside your door. It's the farthest hotel from Banjul, which may not in itself be a bad thing, and offers peace and tranquility for those who like to laze around the pool, or lie out on that golden beach. After dinner entertainment includes dancing to a live band, and there are buffet-style breakfasts and evening meals. Floodlit tennis courts, bicycles for hire, volleyball, windsurfing, sailing, and

Shore fisherman can relax and still catch fish by spending a day at Denton Bridge, just out from the peanut factory. Big fish cruise in the murky waters so you are never sure what you will hit.

surfing are also there to be enjoyed. There is a free sports package for guests including one hour's free tennis, windsurfing, sailing, surfboards, catamaran, and a barbecue once a week. They also do a cooked English breakfast for those of you who get homesick inside 24 hours!

Bank/Currency

The banks in Banjul are open Monday to Thursday 8am to 1pm, but it is just as easy to change your travellers cheques at your hotel. There may also be a currency restriction forbidding you to take the currency, the Dalasis, outside the country. Therefore only change as much as you are going to need each day. The shops are open Monday to Thursday 08.00 to 12.00, and again 14.00 to 17.00, with a half day on Friday and Saturday. The language widely used is English, and the locals speak a language called Wollof, which is totally incomprehensible. I find a mixture of English, hand signals and a fistful of dalasis get me by most times, with the emphasis on the dalasis!

While the fishing should keep you occupied for much of the time, it really is worth getting out and about to see a little of the surrounding countryside. The excursions are not cheap, but they do at least get you out a bit. The Abuko Nature Reserve is a half day tour where you can see antelope, porcupines and monkeys, as well as birds. The Winter '87 price was £5.50. Then there is the two day Tendaba Camp excursion taking you upriver to a camp. This costs £40. Or the 'Roots' tour where you can visit the historic slave trading port on Fort James Island and the fishing village of Albreda, close to Juffure on the north side of the mighty Gambia river. The Bush and Beach tour costs £17, and is well worthwhile. It takes you to some of the native villages, where you will see more children per square yard than anywhere else. They are poorly clothed, and have a friendly innocence that will surely see you parting with something. I advise taking loads of old pens, sweets, paper, anything for kids, and don't make the mistake of giving out all your 'goodies' at the first village. They get the cream of the tourists' freebies, so save some for those less fortunate and farther back from your hotel. Many of the people feel you must not take pictures of them because their soul disappears onto the celluloid. While many are fervent believers in this, for some a few dalasis seem to bring their souls back very quickly. The creek tour is also worth while as you get to see some of the remaining natural birdlife in the massive mangrove areas. Animals like lions, elephants etc have all largely been killed off and eaten, so don't expect a regular safari style tour with any of these trips. They are just excursions, and if I had to choose a couple to go on, I would suggest the bush and beach and creek tour, plus the half day at the Abuko Nature Reserve. Much of the remaining time should be spent in the pursuit of fish.

The Country

Between the months of November and May this small country has the most amazing sunshine record. Many times though there is no real heat in the sun until about 10.30am, and then it dies away at around 3pm. This is due to the particles of sand in suspension high up in the atmosphere from wind storms over the Sahara desert. The effect is that the sunset looks like its starting at 4pm, but it is in fact these sand particles filtering out the sun's rays. During strong sunlight, and particularly on the beach where there may be a cooling breeze blowing, care should be exercised in skin protection. Use at least a factor 8 protection in sunoil or cream, and higher if you are really white of skin. Don't forget to buy a sunscreen lipstick for your lips, as they are painful when burnt.

The months of February, March and April have the longest hours of sunshine, with 9.9 and 10 hours respectively each month. Temperatures during these months can reach 95°F, and the entire summer season from October to April seldom sees it drop much below 90°F. The evenings can be cool, so take appropriate clothing. Much of this slight temperature drop is due to the proximity of the colder Atlantic waters, pleasantly lapping the shoreline.

The Fishing

The fishing of The Gambia has, like so many countries, yet to be exploited. As previously mentioned, the surrounding country of Dakar in Senegal has started what may be one of the best marlin and sailfish areas in the Atlantic. The general coastline of this part of Africa is shallow and riddled with dangerous sandbanks, especially around the area of the Gambia river. Vast quantities of silt are banked up and then moved whenever a gale comes through. Standing on a hotel balcony on a breezy day you can see the white water breaking far out to sea, which is an indication of sandbanks on the bottom, often rising up to within a few feet of the

The ladyfish grow to possibly 30 lbs and represent an excellent fighting fish. Janko Bojang holds this beauty, and the best bait to use would be a whole prawn or shrimp.

Insert: Not a good picture, but a rare shot of a massive and unusual fish taken on a trolled plug from the Gambia river. A kujela, this fish tipped the scales at over a 100 lbs, and will surely be the biggest fish a holiday angler is likely to encounter when river fishing.

surface. The water clarity is therefore impeded by this silt in suspension, making the waters turn from a placid green to a coloured brown. The dropoff, where the depths fall away considerably to form part of the continental shelf and ocean floor proper, is sometimes as far as 20 miles out. Even with a good gameboat, and at the time of writing there are none in The Gambia, it would remain doubtful if the boat owner would want to risk his craft over the changing sandbanks. Once you reach this dropoff the water clarity changes markedly from the green/brown of shallow inshore water, to a rich deep blue. It is here that the big sporting species run, fish like the Atlantic blue marlin, the Atlantic sailfish and the fighting sharks.

Dakar in Senegal has this dropoff a lot closer to their port and consequently they have big game boats that have fast access to this blue water. Further round the coastline the Ivory Coast also has boats that can operate out into the deep water. They now have some of the finest Atlantic blue marlin fishing in the world, with very big billfish going over 500 lbs in weight. Nigeria has, in its city of Lagos, the same potential, and talking with a British ex-patriot who worked out there, it seems as though the fish are ready and waiting to be caught. This coastline has some enormous barracuda hunting in its waters, many found close in to creeks and river estuaries. In fact the world record for the biggest barracuda ever caught on rod and line came from Lagos. The local anglers fish the area from small boats equipped with outboards, and have just started leaving the inshore waters taking an extra fuel tank, to run offshore to the bluewater grounds. What they have discovered is an area of huge Atlantic sailfish, fish up to 100 lbs in weight, which for a species more likely to average about 40 lbs apiece is indicative of what the area has to offer. Apparently the blue marlin often take some of the fish baits used for trolling, but with the anglers using light, 30 lb class tackle for the sailfish, they have lost more marlin than they have landed. Many of these fish have been estimated to weigh in excess of 500 lbs, and the problem is not always light line. If you fight a fish for a long time they reckon you have an excellent chance of getting it 'sharked', though the species they describe to me sounds like a big tiger shark, with a broad flat head. Again these huge sharks are not fished for, as the danger of bringing a live one into a small boat a long way from shore is patently obvious. With so many river deltas and streams from inland running into the sea, I feel these might be huge bull sharks, which have a high tolerance of freshwater, and have even been known to travel miles upstream and attack cattle and humans. They also have a prodigous appetite and a large flat head when viewed from above. Of course until somebody gets out there with some heavy tackle and a suitable craft to fish from, they will never really know. It does however, serve to illustrate just what sort of size these true big fish can achieve. It also indicates, these countries being in the general geographical area of The Gambia, that similar fish are likely to be swimming about in the bluewater off the mouth of the Banjul river.

There are many local fishing villages scattered along the Gambian coastline, with the better and more productive areas being south of the city of Banjul. The further south you go from Banjul and the Gambia river, the cleaner the water becomes, although it still never takes on that deep blue simply because it is not deep enough. On one excursion over the border to the south, we travelled into Senegal. Here at a tourist café I saw a few photographs scattered on the wall. They were of fish, so I naturally took more than a passing interest. There were no boats, but a Frenchman ran a guide service for beach fishing enthusiasts, using a four-wheel drive vehicle to carry both passengers and tackle. He drove them far along those remote beaches to the better fishing spots, and had some very big fish, caught by his clients, strapped across the bonnet of the four-wheel drive. Fish like monster stingrays that surely weighed well over the 100 lbs mark, and a great scrapper when caught on shore tackle. I also saw , pictures of very big sharks that I could not identify. Certainly they were not the mako, blue or hammerhead of the deep ocean waters, but looked like the big brown sand sharks that freqent shallow coloured water. Again, I emphasise the bulk – they were up to at least 200 lbs in weight. As my French was non-existent there was no way I could gain access to any further information, but surely the same sand sharks would feed up around the mouth of the Gambia river where the food would be in a plentiful supply?

Even the small commercial fishing villages in the south had bigger and better catches of a wide variety of fish, and were taken mostly by netting. A long, hardwood boat was launched down the beach, with many hands helping as the weight of these craft must be colossal. The keel appeared to have a thick reinforcement of wood, that was continued out beyond the bow. I assume this was protection against the continual grinding on the sandy beaches as they were both launched and landed, and perhaps for grounding on any of those offshore sandbanks I spoke about. Large forty gallon fuel drums were rolled down the beach, pushed into the water and the boat was sunk. The drum was pushed aboard and the boat quickly baled out to make it float again. An unusual method of loading fuel, and one I had seen nowhere before on my travels. These commercial boats sell any large fish over 5 lbs as soon as they hit the beach, but the smaller fish from half a pound to a pound in weight are cleaned and hung in a thatched roof smoking house to be cured. If you have never been to an African fish smoking house then your nostrils simply haven't lived! I lasted about two minutes inside one, and was amazed to see a couple of locals just lying on the floor waving a palm to keep the worst of the smoke away. I can't imagine their life expectancy is very great.

While the commercials do take the odd big shark and stingray, three species that are a regular product of their work, and highly sought after, are the snappers, ladyfish and barracuda, in that order. Worldwide, many of the snapper species are about the best eating fish you can get, and with the minimum of pollution, they are good and safe to eat. In the westernised areas of the world, heavy industrial pollution is dispensed via the rivers, into the sea, where of course everyone believes it just disappears into the vastness. It doesn't, and starts into the food chain as PCBs and heavy metals like cadmium, low in the life cycle. The shrimps get their dosage of pollution, the small fish eat the shrimps, the big fish eat the small fish. Unfortunately for us, many species of inshore fish are territorial, so they stay inshore ingesting more than their fair share of pollutants. We eat fish and therefore end up with the pollutant inside us, which is why I never or rarely eat UK caught fish. We have too much pollution! Another natural form of poisoning comes from eating barracuda, which in some areas carry the Ciguatera poisoning, getting it from the reef fish they feed on. It is supposed to eventually send you blind and was once prevalent in the Bahamas, where barracuda formed part of the diet. As far as Gambian fish go, they should be reasonably clear of any pollutants and good to eat.

There are a wide variety of snappers in The Gambia ranging from grey snappers, to the highly prized mutton snapper, and bright red snapper. Catching them is best done by using a cube shaped piece of fish bait on or just above the bottom. The best way is by a small livebait, fished on the bottom with a light lead. This is about the only way to take the grey snapper, which is a very wary fish indeed and feeds primarily on tiny reef fish. The ladyfish is one of my favourites, and a very fine fighting fish caught on light tackle. They have an uncanny resemblance to the weakfish, which is an International Game Fishing Association rated gamefish with world record status. Found mainly on the east coast of the United States it is taken in shallow water, right up to the surf coastline by shore anglers and inshore boat anglers. The West African ladyfish looks to me to be not exactly the same fish, but it grows to a size that would blow the world records straight out of the window, as it can top 30 lbs in weight! The best way of taking the ladyfish is from either a drifitng or anchored boat using a size 2 freshwater hook and 12 lb mainline. A 30 lb trace would be advised just in case you hit one of the toothy critturs that abound in the same waters. A whole shrimp is threaded up the shank and dropped down to bump along the bottom. They will take small strips of fish but the shrimps or prawns are far more effective. On hooking one they zig-zag around like a trout and take short hard runs. Excellent to eat, I am not sure whether or not they would respond to groundbaiting with crushed shrimp and fish mixed with sand. It could be that you would simply attract too many smaller fish. They seem to like a few feet of water over their back, so should you decide to shore fish I would wade out to waist deep and then cast out. Of course if you start groundbaiting in the same area you are wading in, you might get a toe nibbled by a shark instead of a ladyfish.

Another small point of interest concerning this species is that way across the other side of this vast continent, in East Africa, I have encountered what I feel is the same species. The Kenya town of Malindi has long been a world centre for Pacific sailfish, and these sailfish come into the dirty water and bluewater edge line to feed on a species of fish called the Malindi herring. This is a fish that feeds in the coloured water that marks the coastline around Malindi, and is caused by the silica crystals and silt washed down from upcountry by the Subaki river. These Malindi herring are I believe exactly the same fish as their cousins on the West African coast, which are in turn possibly the same fish as the weakfish on the East coast of the United States. Should you hook one over 25 lbs, I would suggest photographs and proper weighing with witnesses as it may well be a new unrecognised record for the weakfish. Then we have the barracuda. A piscine hunter of the utmost efficiency, and with a set of dentures that would do justice to a German shepherd dog! The coloured water of the coastline and

Trolling the many creeks that join the main river can be equally successful. The writer took this splendid mutton snapper on a Rapala Magnum plug.

more so in the river itself, means that, like our own Bristol Channel, the mineral contents make the area a haven for young fish to grow in. Wherever there are small fish you are going to have a predator in the chain, and the barracuda is equally at home in the surfline behind the breaking waves, or up in the creeks and mangrove channels that offshoot the Gambia river. While they will take a deadbait or a fish strip fished hard on the bottom, they by far prefer a moving bait, like a livebait or a fast retrieved lure. Lures may only be effective in the sea where the water is a little clearer and they can see better. The best lures for trolling are the Rapala magnums, or those big orange trolling plugs made by Yozuri in Japan. For casting around in the mangrove channels, use either a spoon like the Ryobi *Odin* or the *Toby* series.

If you anchor I suggest you use a piece of shrimp on a size 10 freshwater hook to catch a small live fish, then rehook it on a 2/0 sea hook to a 24in wire trace and one ounce lead. Have your drag set properly as that rush run is a classic for breaking the line of the inexperienced. I feel that, with the large number of small baitfish out in the coloured flow of the main river, there must be a few barracuda swimming about that would top the 40 lb mark. As well as these three main species to go after, there are dozens of weird and wonderful fish up to a couple of pounds that I can give no name to. One has an enormous mouth under its nose, another looks like an angler fish, and many defy description.

The fishing from the beach at the front of the hotels is limited in so far as it really is very shallow. I threw out shrimp and small fish strips on a beachcaster in an effort to find deeper water, and did in fact land two small stingrays. The distance was a good 120 yards, but you don't need to be an expert caster to pick these up. Simply wade out as far as you can then hurl the bait and lead into the distance. If you need a beach rest (I always fish two rods), take in your suitcase a couple of 18in lengths of plastic piping used by

While shore fishing for stingray or ladyfish, why not take an interest in shell collecting? This tropical area hosts a wide variety of sizes and colours.

plumbers, with a diameter of maybe 2in. Saw one end straight across, and saw the other end at a steep angle. This can then be used as a sand spike pushed down into the sand and the rod butt dropped inside the tube. I first saw it used in the States, and naturally it weighs nothing in the suitcase. If you want to fish at night from the front of the hotel beach, make sure you let the gate security man know. He can sit and watch you, thus ensuring your personal safety. Give him a tip of either a few dalasis, or a couple of fish, should you catch anything edible. I think night fishing with a whole fish bait of about eight ounces would pick up those bigger stingray, or maybe even those sand sharks which always feed better during cover of darkness.

If you manage to hire one of the fishing boats from the hotel, try trolling the mangrove channels using those magnum rapala lures. Here the water is slightly cleaner and the predators who hunt visually may give you a take. There is also a species of fish living in the river and surrounding estuary that is definitely worth fishing for. They are called locally the 'Kujela', and resemble something like a cross between a tarpon and a Nile perch. My first encounter with one was when fishing the centre of the Gambia river at a mark known as Dog Island. Here the water is shallow, swirling and full of silt in suspension, carried down from the dry land upstream. The river is up to four miles wide here, and rolls out to sea at a fair pace. To the north is Juffure and Barra, the island being a low lying piece of land used by local river fisherman. Our boatman, Hassan, had a handline with 50 lb line over the stern, baiting his hook with a whole fish. Once, it got broken as a huge unseen fish raced away, the heavy mono thankfully tangled round the engine cowling cover and parted like a pistol shot. I had a couple of fast takes when I fished a whole fish bait on the bottom, but failed to connect with both of them. Live, whole fish seemed a favourite with them, and that didn't surprise me when I saw that cavernous mouth. Perhaps like a tarpon they have a bony plate inside the mouth, into which any hook finds difficulty in taking hold.

I would, in retrospect, consider the best method to fish to be 30 lb boat gear, a running leger with a small live fish for bait, and maybe an ounce of lead to keep it near the bottom, and retain contact in the strong river current. I would advise holding the rod at all times, with the reel in gear and the drag properly set, striking the instant the fish moved off with the bait. Obviously a very sharp hook should be used, and I think this way, although

Huge mangroves, fantastic wildlife, and peace and quiet are what the touring angler finds when he explores the fishing of The Gambia's many creeks.

missing out on the hordes of tiny fish available on light tackle and shrimp bait, you will at least connect with one of these monsters. The largest I have seen (in a picture) that had been taken on rod and line weighed 103 lbs, and was taken by Hassan while trolling with a plug, not in the main river itself, but on the way back to base, and in a mangrove channel.

A good shore mark just about a mile south of the Wadner Beach hotel is a place called Denton Bridge. It can be reached by taking a taxi from outside the front of the hotel, and it overlooks the peanut factory, which is an important part of the Gambian economy. Many locals use handlines to fish it, but it is ideal for either a full day or half day, remembering to take some drinks, food and a towel for the shade. Fishing here is relatively simple. You just rig up a light running leger rig with maybe a one ounce lead, wire trace of two feet and 2/0 hook, baited with a piece of shrimp. You can of course use a piece of fish, and there are plenty of small fish swimming round the bridge supports. Using the shrimp, 6 lb line and a finger nail piece of shrimp you can knock out plenty of bait fish. I have hooked a good few fish from here only to see them disappear out to sea, usually passing the line round a few bridge supports in the process. It is a good mark for the ladyfish, often running into double figures, but they seem to have a habit of taking the tiny baits on the light line. With so many snags around, the argument is very one sided. On a big fish bait, two other friends that have fished Denton Bridge on my advice came back with reports of being broken by big, unstoppable fish. I can't see them being big sharks, but I can see them being big stingrays, moving into this part of river to feed around the mangroves. One of my friends, Paul Harris from the Irish Tourist Board, took my advice and spent a day at Denton Bridge. He saw one of the locals hook a big barracuda on a handline that made a superb piece of nylon knitting with all the other local's lines. It weighed into double figures, and I am quite sure the 'cuda in excess of 25 lbs swim this stretch of water. Eventually we may see a proper charter boat operation using the port Banjul as a base, but until that time you will be forced to explore the fishing potential using whatever means you can. This is very often a far more exciting and satisfying way of doing things, as everything you catch can honestly be considered to be your own.

Any charter boat operation will need to think in terms of a boat at least 30 feet long if they want to venture out to those prolific waters offshore, and carry a substantial piece of navigational equipment such as a SATNAV. Heavy rods and big reels will be the order of the day for the big marlin and shark, plus lighter tackle in the 30 lb class for sailfish. At the moment you will have to try and hire a canoe with outboard and local fisherman, and get him to take you out into the Gambia river, the mangrove creeks, or the oceanside, behind the surfline. Invariably the best way will be to drift using strips of bait or shrimp bumped along the bottom. While I was there a man called Graham Rainer, who previously hailed from Devon, was moored in the Denton Bridge area, doing tours of the Gambia river with his yacht, *The Spirit of Galicia* if I remember correctly. He did have a couple of small open boats and outboards for hire with a guide, and it is worth enquiring at the

Atlantic Hotel if he still has small boats for charter. They will not be able to venture out to sea, but are perfectly adequate for fishing both the mangrove creeks and the main Gambia river. There was a third chance of getting out to the river, in an advert recently being placed in one of the fishing magazines. It was, if I recall correctly, calling itself 'Global Sportfishing', and had a couple of very small boats for hire with tackle etc, and was based at one of the hotels. If you check with your tour operator or rep at the hotel you may learn more about it. In the time between the writing of this book and its publication, somebody may have started a proper charter operation out to the bluewater, but until that time you should be able to find enough exploratory fishing in extremely basic and pleasant surroundings, to make your trip an enjoyable one. The Gambia is a little piece of Africa that many can afford, so with cheap fishing you can have a great time. For more information you can contact: The Gambia Tourist Office, 57 Kensington Court, London, W8. Tel: 01-937-9618.

As this book went to press, a report came in of an exciting new catch of tarpon. This is an IGFA-rated gamefish and is surely the species to put Gambia on the gamefishing map. In the previous few months Mike Benwell, who runs the *Sportfisher* I and II boats had lost many big tarpon, some estimated to weigh 200 lbs. Two fish have now been landed by him, weighing 130 lbs and 140 lbs. They were taken trolling with artificial lures. Hopefully we will now learn more about the tarpon's movements – I believe they may well use the Gambia river for spawning purposes. These trips are organised through Global Sportfishing (address advertised in the fishing press).

IRELAND

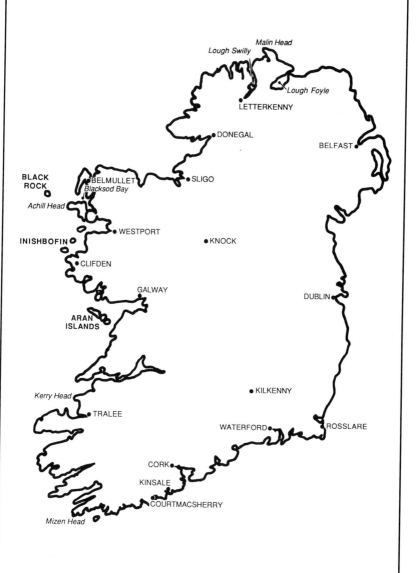

IRELAND

Travel Tips

Access

There are two ways to reach Ireland from Britain. You can either fly into one of the airports and connect with a tour operated bus system, or hire a car and drive yourself. The other way is by sailing from one of the many different points of departure, and either hire a car, or simply take your own. Many operators run frequent flights to Ireland, among them Aer Lingus, British Airways, British Midland Airways, Brymon Airways, Dan-Air, Longanair, Manx Airlines and Ryanair. These airlines operate duty free facilities on most routes, and services are from Britain to Dublin, Cork, Shannon and Waterford. There are also a wide range of promotional fares to choose from, with Ryanair offering infants free passage on their Dublin route. For a self-drive motoring holiday book your car with you flight. There are savings to be made with Aer Lingus 'Super Drive' or British Airways and Dan Air Fly/Drive programmes. Subject to government approval additional air services may be operated in 1988 to various points in Ireland by carriers such as British Air Ferries, Euroair, Malinair, Ryanair, Shannon Executive Aviation and Virgin Atlantic Airways. The choice of air services appears to be growing rapidly and opens up many new areas quickly to the travelling angler.

If you decide to travel by sea there is ease of access to the various ferryports by Britain's motorway system, also coach and rail services. Both Sealink and B & I operate an integrated fare structure. Fares are uniform on all their routes to Ireland except Liverpool to Dublin which is about 15% more expensive due to the longer sea route taken. The routes are as follows:

Fishguard/Rosslare. Passenger and drive-on/drive-off car ferry sailings operated jointly be Sealink and B & I line. Sailing time: 3½ hours.

Holyhead/Dun Laoghaire. Regular drive-on/drive-off car ferry and passenger services by Sealink. Sailing time: 3½ hours.

Holyhead/Dublin. Regular drive-on/drive-off car ferry and passenger services operated by B & I line. Sailing time: 3½ hours.

Liverpool/Dublin. Passenger and drive-on/drive-off car ferry services operated by B & I line. Sailing time: 8 hours.

Isle of Man/Dublin. The Isle of Man Steam Packet Company runs seasonal passenger and drive-on/drive-off car ferry sailings, mid-May to mid-September with B & I line acting as agents. Sailing time: 4 1/2 hours. Inter-City Ireland also operate a fast, air-conditioned through rail service connecting at all ports with shipping services to Ireland, and onward services with CIE throughout Ireland. Full details can be found in the Inter-City Ireland brochure, *Rail and Sea to Ireland*, which is available at travel agents and railway stations throughout Britain.

Rail-Sail-Drive is also available from main tour operators at very attractive rates. Transalpino/Eurotrain offers discounted fares to several destinations in Ireland for young people under 26.

Express Coach Services are available from Britain to various cities and towns in Ireland. Superbus have regular departures at over 90 destinations. Tickets for this service are available at over 3000 National Express agents in the UK, and at all National Coach Stations.

Planned New Service. A proposed new route covering Swansea/Cork may be in operation by 1988. For details contact Swansea/Cork Car Ferries Ltd, tel: (0792) 456116, your travel agent or the nearest Irish Tourist Board Office for further information.

The Country

The traveller will find the pace of life slow in Ireland. Its people are almost a portion of the country and its historic past, working their way through the day steadily until they reach the hour when it is time to drink and chat. Ireland and its history make a visit compelling, where in the bars animated Irishmen gather to tell tales and drink the black Guinesss until all around are happy. Failte, the Gaelic word for welcome is everywhere, for these pleasant people are not only concerned with the monetary income from tourism, but they really do seem to have time to chat to you a stranger. They are renowned for their hospitality, whether its the welcome of the farmhouse, or in front of a crackling fire in the safety of a luxurious castle set in the timeless countryside. The landscape is untouched by industrial pollution, its freshwater rivers tinkling through the woods and across fields with fish

For the touring angler in Ireland, nothing can match the pastel colours of a trip through the Connemara Mountains. With almost as much water as sky, it is a photographer's dream, the solitude finding a relaxation difficult to pinpoint in any other place. This is County Galway. Doorway to a fisherman's paradise.

everywhere. The roads are free from heavy traffic allowing carefree driving in many of the country lanes. Or you can explore at your leisure in a horse-drawn caravan the natural beauty of the countryside. For those who simply love messing about on the river you can become your own skipper on the mighty river Shannon.

This contains the largest area of inland waterways in Ireland or Britain, where you can travel for up to 140 miles, taking in fishing or swimming along the way. For those who require the 'real thing', you are never more than a day's drive from the sea, that vast Atlantic Ocean which has carved some of the most fantastic scenery along the west coast. Much of Ireland, its countryside, its people are unchanged by the passage of time. A trip spent fishing here will surely see you long to return.

Accommodation

Accommodation can be reserved through the area's two Tourist Information Offices. One is in Letterkenny, tel: (074) 21160; the other is the Sligo Tourist Information Office, tel: (071) 61201. The Tourist Board, or Bord Failte is officially responsible for grading and registration of visitors' accommodation in the country. They can book you at hotels, guesthouses, Irish homes, farmhouses, or caravan and camping parks. There are some seasonal offices open during peak tourist times as follows:

Bundoran Tourist Information Office. Tel: (072) 41350. Open June 1st to 15th September.

Carrick-on-Shannon Tourist Information Office. Tel: (078) 20170. Open May to September.

Donegal Town Tourist Information Office. Tel: (073) 21297. Open June to September.

Dungloe Tourist Information Office. Tel: (075)21297. Open June to August.

Banking services are available in all cities and towns throughout Ireland. Banks are open from 10.00 to 12.30 hours and 13.30 to 15.50 hours, Monday to Friday. In Dublin the banks stay open until 17.00 hours on Thursdays. There are bicycles for hire in Ardara town and Donegal town for those anglers wishing to reach more obscure stretches of coastline that the car cannot reach.

Donegal

The best of the sea fishing in Ireland is to be found all along its western coastline. Rugged cliffs, open wide beaches, or 'strands' as they are known, provide the shore angler with a huge potential. From many of the quaint fishing ports the more ambitous can charter a deep sea vessel, which together with a local boatman who knows the waters like the back of his hand, and a little lady luck, even the beginner can hope to catch good fish. This part of Ireland's coastline is warmed by the North Atlantic drift. A finger of that warm water artery, the Gulfstream, stretches right up from the eastern seaboard of the United States, to trickle its rich ocean current tantalisingly past Ireland's shoreline. It is this, coupled with the mild airflow that makes for those mild or 'soft' days of south-westerly ocean breezes and drizzling rain. To be fair, the good fishing starts in the north, in County Donegal. An area of great contrasts. It has long been popular as a holiday destination. It presents an ever-changing spectacle of landscapes and seascapes set against a backdrop of moors and mountains, with evidence everywhere of the old Irish culture and traditions. Its geology is interesting as the Caledonian mountain system extends from Scandinavia right into Donegal and gives a strong north-east to south-west grain to the mountains. The result is a mountain barrier ranging down from the weather station at Malin head in the extreme north to Ballyshannon and Bundoran in the south. Fishermen have always plied their trade in these treacherous waters – archeological discoveries show that the inlets of north Donegal were used as far back as 7000 B.C. in the Irish Mesolithic period, by a hunting and fishing people. The towns and villages all have at the very least one bar, a few shops and a petrol station, which together with the accommodation is basically all you need for a good fishing trip.

Fishing in Donegal

It is best to approach each section of Ireland's excellent fishing by dividing it into two types, the shore fishing and the deep sea fishing. For shore fishing there is no restriction on fishing from rocks, beaches or estuaries for any species of sea fish, but a license is required for salmon and sea trout. With deep sea fishing you are governed purely by the accessibility of the better spots, and the need for shelter from bad seas, in the shape of a harbour, natural or man made.

Starting with the shore fishing in the north, the pier head at Rathmullan in Lough Swilly is probably one of the safest shore marks to fish for codling, thornback rays and flounder. Using a big fish bait legered straight out in the tide run there is an excellent chance of a tope. The rays average 5 lbs in weight, and occasionally mackerel run up into the bay. Virtually any access you can find down to the water line at Fanad Head will be productive for wrasse, dogfish and conger. It's rough ground so you will have to use expendable weights like spark plugs. Try spinning for mackerel, pollock and coalfish. Beware of any seas with the wind in the north as treacherous swells can push twenty feet up the rocks. Always fish with a friend and take a rope for safety.

Moving west you have the steep shingle beach of Glashagh strand which is rocky on the eastern side and clean ground at the west. It fishes best after a westerly gale providing codling on lugworm. Much of this is rocky shoreline and therefore suitable country for both wrasse and pollock. Following the coast along to the west you come to Downings which is a small resort with hotel and pub, and sporting a fine curved beach that looks out into Sheephaven Bay. It has a small pier from which you can catch rays, flounders, and at high water in the summer, the mullet move in close. The boat fishing from here is mainly outside the security of the Lough, running way out to Tory Island. Drifting to the north of the island over the rough ground, sport can be excellent with big cod, pollock, gurnard and the occasional turbot. The latter run well into double figures, and are generally taken from the scrubby ground in between the rocks. I would think that Sheephaven Bay holds tope during the months of May and June, as back in Lough Swilly these fine sporting fish run the bay during these months and average over 25 lbs apiece.

Charter boats are limited here, but Jim Deevey, the proprietor of the Rathmullan Hotel may be able to book you one of the better Swilly boats like the *Pegasus* owned by Mac Bowden. A contact for a deep sea vessel could be found at the Downings Hotel, as most of the boats come from other tiny fishing villages across Sheephaven Bay. Once you move around the coast to the western shore you face the full Atlantic swell, and as the area is primarily all rock fishing, care must be exercised in climbing to and from the fishing platforms. Always travel in pairs and take a rope.

A few of the better shore marks between Derrybeg and Ardara are as follow. At Derrybeg Estuary, lugworm and white ragworm can be dug for bait from the bank edges of the channel. At Bunbeg harbour you can try floatfishing from the quay at high water for mullet, that have been prebaited with bread or fish, prior to fishing. At night a mackerel bait fished on the bottom may produce a conger eel. At Termon, which is a headland just south west of Dungloe there is spinning for pollock and mackerel from the rocks. Both floatfishing and paternostering with either lugworm or crab on the bottom give wrasse, while a very long cast should put you over sand and into the domain of the flounder. Further south at Ardara you can dig fresh worms at Barkillew, with lugworm, white ragworm and clam obtainable opposite Lambe's Island. There are crabs in the weed on the channel bank and they can be used to good effect if they are in the 'peeler' conditions for big flounders. The two fishing spots are at Loughros point with bottom fishing for conger and dogfish, plus spinning for pollock, mackerel and coalfish. The other is at Ranny Point North which is just west of Ardara town, where the Owenea river channel gives ground fishing for flounder and eels. There are tackle shops in the towns of Dungloe, Glenties and Ardara.

This is a prime deep sea area that has yet to be fully exploited by rod and line sportfishing due to the lack of protective harbours and charter boat facilities. Much of the north of this Donegal sea has superb potential for wreck fishing, and reef fishing, so hopefully in time the facilities here will improve. Moving south again we come to Killybegs, very much a commercial fishing port where the huge ships that harvest the mackerel and herring stocks through winter moor up to unload. It still looks very much like a Victorian village built around an adequate deep water fishing harbour, and the fleet unloading their holds of fish means there is little problem in procuring some bait. In the harbour lurk some tremendous conger eels, waxing fat on the easy pickings from the fish spilled from these super trawlers. Night fishing is best for them, but take strong tackle, as they have been landed to over 40 lbs.

Another good shore spot for wrasse, conger and pollock is St. John's point. Facing Sligo bay it has a long finger of rock jutting out into the water and offering at least several vantage points of comfort during westerly or easterly winds. There is a charter boat available here, the *Niamh Og,* 36 feet in length and skippered by local boatman Enda O'Callahan. He can take you out into deeper water for pollock or conger most months of the year, depending on the weather of course! In the months of June to September he can also take you on a drift in the bay for blue shark, the largest he has taken being over 100 lbs in weight. The bay here is extensive and moving a few miles to the east you come to Donegal town. Situated at the estuary of the river Eske that flows from Lough Eske into Donegal Bay, it is on the junction of the N56 and N15. Lugworm can be dug to the east of the local golf club, and the only other sport would be the mullet fishing from the quays at high water. Groundbaiting in advance increases your chances of success considerably, and mullet have also been taken by flyfishing. Take the N15 south and you come to Ballyshannon, a town which winds up a steep hill above the waters of the River Erne. It has always been a centre of importance for its river crossing and there were striking river falls at Assaroe which have now been muted by hydro-electric development. There is some good shore fishing in the estuary away from the town in the Erne estuary for sea trout which can be taken spinning, and flounders which can be taken bottom fishing. Optimum time is two hours either side of low water. The best of the Donegal Bay shore fishing comes as you move out of the bay itself and towards the deeper waters of the Atlantic. Some excellent shark fishing is available in the next county, which produces many top Irish sea fish.

County Sligo

Is a maritime area of extraordinary beauty and vivid contrast in its lakes and forests, mountains and rivers. Its landscape is a result of processes which have gone on for many hundreds of millions of years. The Ox mountains contain the oldest rocks found in the area, some 600 million years old. The layers of rocks which make up the mountains have been relatively unchanged by the wind and weather, leaving them with their characteristic flat-topped appearance. It is a county rich in the quality and quantity of its historic and archaeological remains, giving the hilltop wanderer plenty of scope for a vivid imagination in recounting the lives of the Tomb People who lived there perhaps as early as 4000 B.C. Sligo town itself is a flourishing commercial, industrial and marketing centre, being the largest town in the north-west, with a population of over 18,000.

Donegal-Leitrim-Sligo tourism offers a year-round tourist

information office at Temple Street, Sligo, tel: (071) 61201. There are also tourist information points at Killorans Traditional Restaurant, Tubbercurry, and at Maughan's, Inniscrone. They can also book you in any of the range of approved accommodation which includes hotels, guesthouses, town and country homes, holiday homes and caravan parks. There is a daily air service between Dublin and Sligo airport (Strandhill), which operates from Monday to Friday. For the rail traveller there are three services daily between Dublin and Sligo on weekdays, and twice on Sundays throughout the year.

Fishing in Sligo

To the west of Killala bay lies some excellent shore fishing marks, reached by driving north from Killala town towards Rathlackan. Just outside Killala is Ross beacon. This area offers the shore angler spinning in the channel for sea trout, and bottom fishing with baits for flounder and the occasional conger eel. In contrast to the rock fishing there is Farrellstown Strand to the north which is a superb beach offering not only flounder, but the chance of a turbot as well by fishing small fish strip baits on a flood tide. Near the town of Rathlackan there is a good spot for bait near the town. Lugworm are available on both banks of the estuary channel, and sandeel can be scraped near the waterline of the same channel.

Suitably armed with bait there are three top marks to fish. Lackan Pier offers comfortable fishing for a wide variety of species including mackerel, pollock and coalfish that can be taken spinning. Floatfishing yields some small wrasse on lugworm baits, flounders, move across the sandy patches and the odd conger will pick up a fish bait legered over rough ground. Moving further north you have a mark called Cannalickada, which is a rock climbing area but offers pollock, conger, coalfish and wrasse. For legering baits hard on the bottom I find it best to use either an old spark plug or an expendable weight like a nut or stone as the bottom is very snaggy and rough. To the north-west lies Downpatrick head, with an impressive view out across the bay, and cliff fishing for pollock, wrasse, coalfish and conger. Its best fished from the eastern side, and access can be difficult, possibly dangerous when the rocks are wet from rain. Exercise caution.

By taking the N59 into Killala we have crossed into another county, Mayo, but of course the fish don't know the boundary lines

What a catch! The writer had shown the skipper and anglers how to catch the fighting pollock using just a single redgill artificial sandeel. They took this 350 lb catch fishing from the west coast of Ireland out from Blacksod Lighthouse.

between the counties. They may, however, possibly know that County Mayo is one of the leading centres of deep sea fishing frequented by both British and European anglers.

County Mayo

A section of the country where the force of the Atlantic makes deep inroads into its coastline on the west and north. The county does not boast many high mountains but those that are there achieve drama by isolation, whether it is the fabled holy mountain of Croagh Patrick (765 metres), or Croagham (668 metres) in Achill, whose cliffs plunge down almost vertically to the roaring Atlantic. Parts of Mayo, particularly those of Belmullet and the north-east of the county can be as thinly populated as anywhere. A blanket fog rolling in from the sea can offer a stunning silence, the peace shattered only by an alarmed snipe or grouse.

Although the shore fishing is not at its best in Mayo, it is more due to the difficult access to some of the outer rock marks, than the lack of the species themselves. However, the boat fishing is excellent and starts in the north of Mayo at a town called Ballina. This is an attractive town on the river Moy and is the largest in County Mayo. It has some traces of the elegance one associates with a planned 18th century town, which to some extent it was, being founded by Lord Tyrawley in 1730. There is a pleasant walk by the Moy, where in season, the salmon run. There is a seasonal tourist office in Ballina, tel: (096) 22422, which is open from early July to the end of August, Monday to Saturday 10.00 hours to 18.00 hours. The County Mayo office which is open all year round is: Westport Tourist Information Office, The Mall, Westport, tel: (098) 25711, hours Monday-Friday 09.00-17.15. There is no lunch closing time during June to September inclusive.

There is a selection of tackle shops throughout the area, the main one being in Ballina: John Walkin, Tone Street, Ballina, tel: (096) 22422. Here you can also enquire about booking one of the charter boats, the best being the Tourist Board approved 36 foot *Cleona*, which is fully equipped to take anglers either bottom fishing or shark fishing. Some of the other County Mayo fishing tackle shops are as follows: J. Byron, Arran Street, Ballina; Thomas Collins, Castle Street, Castlebar; John Comer, Main Street Swinford; Frank Clarke, King's Hill, Westport; Brendan Jones, Main Street, Foxford; J. Munnelly, Main Street, Crossmolina and P.J. McGee, Sandymount, Newport.

Fishing in Mayo

From Ballina, a drive west through Crossmolina and Bangor will see you in Belmullet, one of the most popular venues for sea fishing in Europe. Although there is potential for shore sport all along the western shoreline of the mullet peninsula, there are only two real possibilities that I have found to provide really consistent sport. Ballyglass lighthouse is reached by a gravel road, where you can park on the hillside just outside the perimeter wall. Here you can climb down the rocks and fish into Broadhaven Bay for mackerel and pollock on the spinner, or cast out a large piece of mackerel and await a conger or ray. By fishing the base of the lighthouse you will find many rock gullies that are excellent for catching wrasse on paternostered lugworms or hardback crab. Another good technique for catching bigger pollock is to use a redgill artificial sandeel cast out into the tidal flow with two ounces of lead, and retrieved over the top of the kelp beds. Just to the west of this lighthouse, and visible from the rocks is one of the prettiest surf beaches I have had the privilege to fish. Known as Pollacoppal it produces only flounders, the odd dog fish, and seatrout. A pleasure to fish when a strong breeze puts the surf up, it should produce rays to the angler prepared to put in a few hours during the night.

For the easiest walk to a fishing mark you need look no further than Ballyglass Pier. A tiny structure with a high wall one side and old Irish trawlers the other, it has a reputation for producing the conger if not in size, then certainly in numbers. Fishing just off the end you simply lower a piece of mackerel fillet down to the bottom with a spark plug weight and you can usually get a take from a conger around high water. If they do fail to bite you have huge mullet that swim round the boats, and take tiny pieces of mackerel, or you can spin for coalfish and pollock. The fishing is decidedly better in the autumn months when the mackerel come in close enough to shore to be taken on the float, while distance casting with a mackerel fillet will put the bait in the deeper main channel where both dogfish and good thornback rays should intercept it.

In the town square of Belmullet there is a shoe shop called Valkenburgs. Its owner, one Buddy Valkenburg, will be your best source of information as to the best charter boat to book, and the best shore mark to try. For the floatfishing enthusiast there are good mullet to be caught in the harbour to the back of Buddy's shop, but the first few hours of flood appear to be the best time, with bread being the premier bait. Down the mullet peninsula there is Elly Bay where big seatrout are reputed to take chunks of mackerel cast into the surf. I have yet to catch one but have heard it said from enough different people to think it is certainly worth a session. This is the main Atlantic beach, and Elly waters have a strong tide run so a grip lead may be required. Down the top of the mullet peninsula lies Blacksod lighthouse. Fishing from the end of the pier over high water in the autumn months it is possible to take conger and dogfish on mackerel baits, while the mackerel themselves sometimes come into the pier and can be taken on the spinner. Drop in to see the lighthouse keeper there, Vincent Sweeney. He has a great knowledge of all the deep water marks and can point you in the right direction as regards a good shore mark or two.

Although the Belmullet charter boats mostly work out into Broadhaven Bay, I feel the better fishing for bigger fish is to be had in the deep water out around the Inishkea Islands and Achill head. Pollock abound in the deep water tangled with its underwater reefs and rocks, taking anything from a string of

The magic peace of fishing Ireland's prolific waters is seen here as a fisherman tries his like for a fighting tope in Blacksod Bay. Given good weather, there are few places in Europe to surpass the sport of the Emerald Isle.

feathers to a carefully presented rubber sandeel. The fishing for this species at a mark out from the Inishkeas has seen us take as much as 500 lbs of fish, mainly pollock, but with a few cod thrown in for good measure. If the weather is fine and the breeze light you can steam right out to the blackrock, a lighthouse that stands sentinel in the Atlantic, whose reefs and currents provide the bigger fish with as much food as they want. Blue sharks run to specimen size, the largest I ever saw weighed 110 lbs, although Porbeagles that have yet to be fished for undoubtedly run larger. In Blacksod Bay, on the sheltered side of the mullet peninsula, swim huge monkfish to over 50 lbs, tope to nearly the same weight, bull huss and skate. The water is like some vast shallow lake, and from May to September is full of fighting fish that give great sport on light tackle. Mackerel is the best bait for boat fishing, but the shore angler has more than enough dried-out bays to dig his lugworm when the tide goes out. One of the latest new boats to ply these waters for the tourist is owned by Mickey Lavelle. He runs a petrol station and garage repair service just a mile from Blacksod lighthouse and will eagerly drop what he is doing to take you out fishing. You can get in touch with Mickey by dropping in to see Buddy Valkenburg, as he seems to have an intimate knowledge of who is working where, and on what day.

In contrast to the peaceful, yet almost lonely plains of the mullet peninsula area, you can drive south to Westport. This is a gem of a town, planned to be an adjunct to Westport house, which is a notable Georgian mansion. It still remains a fine town with a canalised river and 18th-century bridge. The fishing here is also more biased to the boat anglers with the hundreds of islands in Clew Bay affording great scenery and superb fishing. With such shallow water and so many islands present there is plenty of tidal flow to bring in the bigger fish like tope and monkfish. Skate, bull huss and other species swarm into Clew Bay during the summer and autumn months giving the boat angler as much in the way of diverse sport as he can handle. The actual sea area of Clew Bay is vast and therefore presents the shore angler with a large perimeter of shoreline to fish and find the species he is after. In the south-west corner of the bay lies Carrownisky Strand. Here you can take flounders, small turbot and the occasional bass, while distance casting during calm spells will put you in touch with the rays. Moving back east there is a stony reef at Bertraw Strand where spinning can give up both seatrout and bass, by casting and working the lure on the westerly facing beach. From the point it is possible to hook a tope while bottom fishing with mackerel strip bait, and in the deep slack water pool behind Bertraw Island, ray and monkfish may also be encountered. At Rossmoney, slightly north-west of Westport there is a good mark for the distance casters in search of bigger fish than the usual flounders. By walking 200 yards to the right of the pier there is a large rocky outcrop. Fish just inside this over the mudflat and you could see yourself attached to a big bull huss or conger eel. It's a low water mark, so fish it about two hours down and two hours up for best results.

Further round Clew Bay at Mullaranny there is beach fishing on the strand for a mixed bag of dogfish, turbot, ray flounder and the occasional bass. Some specimen bass have also been recorded here. From the pier you can take mackerel and small pollock by spinning, and floatfishing with either lugworm or hardback crab produces wrasse. Drive west along the coast road and you come to Corraun. Here there are various places to shore fish, with high water being the optimum period, and the usual wrasse, conger and pollock being taken. While County Mayo offers the adventuring angler a rugged backdrop of scenery, the next area down the Irish coast is a little softer on the eyes.

County Galway

This is Ireland's second largest county with an area of nearly 6000 square kilometres. It is an area of amazing contrasts, and dominates the very heart of the west coast mainly because it has a thriving city of ancient origin. It is also the centre of departures for tourists travelling to view the Aran islands and that glorious area of colour and heather, the Connemara mountain. It is an extensive Gaelic speaking area, and has the Lough Corrib, world famous for its wild brown trout fishing. The geological history of the county is still not yet fully understood. The oldest rocks in the county are those exposed in the central Connemara area, for example in the Maamturk Mountains, the Twelve Pins, and westwards to Clifden. Galway City, which gave its name to the surrounding county, is a former Norman settlement and medieval trading post. The area of this coastline has many intrusions by the scouring winds and Atlantic Ocean, with the result that, while boat fishing in the area is undoubtedly very good, facilities and ports are few.

Fishing in Galway

The main fishing area is centered around Clifden, and here several boats may be enquired after. The Tourist Board approved craft is the *Blue Lynx,* 35 feet long and bookable through John Ryan, Sky Road, Clifden, tel: (095) 21384. Anchoring is a rarity in boat fishing here, yet it would open up a whole new door for modern techniques to be tried. The average Irish charter skipper will want to drift over rough ground so as not to lose his anchor, but anchoring over sand and shingle often produces better fishing. However the species you are likely to contact in a June to September period would be blue shark, conger, rays, gurnard, mackerel, pollock coalfish and cod. The water is not particularly deep, so you have to steam the boat outside the main body of land before there is any appreciable drop in depth. The shore fishing offers great chances for those willing to explore all those estuaries and channels cut through the rock strata. The best is located just outside the town of Clifden, driving westwards on the southern side of the channel. There is a mark with an obelisk daymark called the White Lady which offers superb bottom fishing for rays. The most I have taken with two other anglers beachcasting fillets of mackerel from the rocks below the White Lady was seventeen. I hasten to add that they were kept alive in rock pools, photographed and returned alive to the water. This must be a area for a big shore tope as well, provided you fish a big bait a long way out. Moving south west from here there is a small boat harbour from which you can take wrasse by float fishing or paternostering a lugworm on the bottom during a flood tide.

Just round the headland from here are two more good shore marks. The first you reach is Ballinaga which fishes on a flood tide for wrasse and rays. Then a little further on is Candoolin which responds to lighter tackle and worm baits for flounder, plaice and small turbot. The same species abound all round the small beaches and coves of Mannin Bay, while plenty of lugworm can be collected at Doonloughan, Candoolin, Clifden and inside Omey Island. To the north west of Clifden there is a vast area of as yet, undiscovered shore fishing, but a mark worth trying is Omey island, on the south western tip. Spinning and bottom fishing will give you a chance of pollock, wrasse and conger. Moving north around the headland again there is a mark at Aughrusbeg which is good ground for spinning either using the Ryobi Odin lures or small redgill sandeel for mackerel and pollock.

The potential of both shore and boat fishing is great indeed, but I would say to those anglers interested in more than just catching fish to take a knapsack, a rod, reel and bait and explore the shoreline for yourself. The hotel in Clifden is fine, and there is all kinds of accommodation in the shape of hotels, country homes, guesthouses, farm houses and caravan and camping areas throughout the county. It is serviced by an efficient network of national routes, from Limerick in the south to Sligo in the north. Most roads lead direct into Galway City and from there access can be had to either Connemara or the west coast. There is a direct rail route from Dublin to Galway, and good bus services from most of the major towns in Ireland. Connemara has a national park, and Galway has many different restaurants to dine at. The Galway Tourist Information Office is open all year round, at Aras Failte, Eyre Square, tel: (091) 63801. Hours Monday to Saturday 09.00-18.00. July to August 09.00-19.00. There are also seasonal tourist offices open from July to August in Salthill, Tuam, Clifden and Ballinasloe. All have a guide to Tourist Board approved accommodation. Several shops sell a limited amount of tackle and they are as follows:

Galway: Hugh Duffy, 5 Mainguard Street; Galway City Sports, Eglington Street; T. Naughton & Sons, 35 Shop Street.
Ballinasloe: Keller Bros. at Portumna; Mr. Garry Kenny, Palmerstown Stores.
Clifden: Wallace, in the Main Street.

If you want to try something really different in the way of exploring then you really must take the small cattle boat ferry or fishing smack to the island of Inishbofin. You catch it from the tiny village of Cleggan, and it takes about half an hour to get out to the tiny natural harbour that is its only shelter. One hotel operates there, and is managed and owned by Margaret Murray, one of the nicest people I have met. Her son Michael runs a fishing boat there and is willing to take you on a tour of the other islands, or you can dip a line and see what species you come up with. It is sparsely populated and a dream to walk over on a fine day, from a tiny lily fringed freshwater pool in a vale, to the edge of the western cliffs that plunge into the churning Atlantic. The shore spinning for mackerel, coalfish and big pollock is nothing short of fantastic and I have no hesitation in stating that it is simply the best I have ever experienced. Literally any deep water close to the rock outcrops is worth trying, and I add as a spice to any shore angler that I feel there might be the possibility of a shark from the shore here. From the boat, you have tremendous thornback ray fishing, not particularly large fish but certainly present in numbers. There are small eyed rays, conger, turbot, gurnard, cod, pollock and jumbo sized dabs all present for the boat angler and all within sight of the hotel. You could almost hold up a fish for Margaret to see in the hotel so that she can warm up the frying pan! The true excitement of adventure lies in exploring the deeper water outside the islands where both blue and porbeagle shark, possibly big halibut and certainly tope swim. An island holiday of three or four days will find you having difficulty returning from the paradise tranquility of Inishbofin.

County Kerry

A ridge of purple hazed mountains in the south-west corner of Ireland. They stab westwards into the Atlantic like the talons of an eagle, spines of hard rock separated by drowned valleys, and warm air everywhere. From the Dingle peninsula, long famous for its superb bass fishing to the Ring of Kerry, a popular tourist trail, down to the Beara peninsula, is possibly the prettiest land in all Europe, and untouched by commerce and industry. Fishing in County Kerry is fishing as it should be. Silent. Pure. Clean... and damn good! The coastline is spectacular, being liberally sprinked with antiquities, fortresses whose chief defender now is the sea, and lonely castles standing guard over coves and inlets which nobody visits but the lobster fishers. It was the area of hermits, none with a more spectacular hermitage than Skellig Michael, a 700 foot tooth of near vertical rock that jabs out of the tumultuous ocean nine miles off the Ring of Kerry. Up near the summit a tiny community of monks endured for centuries, living in beehive shaped huts and worshipping in a tiny church. It is anyone's guess how they managed to survive, but fish and puffins must have formed most of their diet.

Kerry has a personality. A shifting balance of light, water, mountain and bog which in turn influences its people. A dull sea mist can suddenly disperse to reveal brilliant, breathtaking colours. The very mood of the mountains can change with the clouds, but the rocks remain as inert as on the day they were born. The Dingle peninsula was formed by great climatic changes and vast geological upheavals between 400 and 200 million years ago. It has the highest mountains in Ireland. Peaks like Macgillycuddy Reeks above Killarney, and Mount Brandon above Dingle range are around 3000 metres high, but they are weather worn stumps of great mountains. Millions of years ago Kerry was once part of a great burning desert reduced by sun and rain to sand, then sunk into the sea to make limestone, then forced up yet again to be a tropical jungle that forms the coal measures of today. It is interesting to learn that as little as 7000 years ago the county was attached to the European mainland, and along this bridge, now mainly under the Bay of Biscay, travelled those Mediterranean plants that are now such an engaging part of Kerry.

For the fisherman visiting Kerry there is a wealth of accommodation, registered and approved by Bord Failte. Hotels, guest houses, farmhouses, town and country homes, plus the more unusual for those with rambling ways such as horse drawn caravans, youth hostels and camping parks. There are year round Tourist Information offices at Killarney, tel: (064) 31633 and at Tralee, tel: (066) 21288. Seasonal offices operate during the June to September period in Ballybunion, Dingle, Caherciveen, Kenmare and tourist points at Sneem and Killorglin. The county is linked to other areas by a good rail network out of Dublin and Cork, and there are major airports at Cork and Shannon. Two continental car ferries serve the county from the ferryport at Ringaskiddy near Cork City. Kerry is also linked to county Clare by a car ferry at Tarbert and there is also a small airport at Farranfore. There is a good bus service run by CIE to many parts of the county, and full details can be obtained from one of the tourist information offices.

Fishing in Kerry

The shoreline, littered as it is with so many strands, creeks and inlets, is a shore fisherman's dream come true, for if the sea is too flat to put up a good bass surf on the strands, it will be ideal for some climbs down to a rocky outcrop and some sport with the wrasse. Alternately should the wind whip up, which it can do often down in the south-west, then rock fishing will be dangerous, but a good creaming surf on a wide bass strand will give you sport with flounder, turbot, plaice and the much prized bass. The boat fishing must be superb in the deep water offshore, but the many charter boats tend to work close in to the shoreline, or in the big bays of shallow water.

Starting in the north of Kerry some of the better fishing spots are as follows. About four miles north of Ballybunion there are two fine surf beaches at Littor Strand and Beal Strand. Both fish best in a wind when there is a surf up and the species likely to be encountered by bottom fishing with lugworm bait would be bass, turbot and plaice. At Ballybunion town there is good bass fishing, while over the rough ground at Blackrock, slightly south of the town, you can expect bass, flat fish, conger, pollock and wrasse. Moving south again past the golf links there are various sports to try for the bass and flatfish as the rough ground gives way to surf fishing. Here you may barely see another as far as the eye can see, and it really is a joy to fish. A flood tide is best with peeler crab, sandeel or lugworm being the top three baits. As for the collection of bait, lugworm can be dug at low water from Littor Strand, and Cashen Estuary on Beal Strand, cockles can also be collected here for bait, and are very good for flatfish. Mackerel are always difficult to catch from an open surf beach, so try a fillet of small pollock, which has been used successfully for tope.

The peninsula farther south at Kerry Head is both impressive to fish and difficult to climb down to. The last time I fished here was with Kevin Linnane of the Central Fisheries Board, and we were wrasse fishing. I seem to remember struggling to catch half a dozen small wrasse, while both Kevin and fellow sea angling officer Norman Dunlop hammered out about 50 wrasse (averaging 3 lbs) between them. It was a valuable lesson. If you go to Kerry Head wrasse fishing, take just one rod, a lot of lugworm and plenty of spare leads. It really can be super sport on light tackle, but take great care in climbing down, and respect the prevailing sea conditions. Pollock and mackerel can both be taken by spinning with a redgill and two ounce weight in the deep water here. There is no harbour facility so the boat fishing is non existent. The top of Kerry Head is peat bog, so if you drive up onto it, keep to the tracks and do not drive off the road without getting out and testing the road beforehand.

Moving back round south from Kerry Head you come to Ballyheige, which on a flood tide offers good bass and flatfish sport. All along here is a massive sweeping open strand, a vast plain of white sand and spuming water that could lose a thousand beach anglers. Small strips of mackerel will be intercepted by turbot, while lugworm fished on a very light leger will take plaice, flounder and bass. At the back of the next town south, Fenit island, there is a mark known as Round Castle. From here on legered mackerel strip you can take good thornback ray on the flood tide. Yet don't forget the bass and sea trout that will have run past you up into Barrow Harbour. On an ebb tide they will be coming back out again and can be taken by spinning. Barrow Harbour itself is primarily a high water mark, but gives some flounder, plaice and occasional bass. It is a far better place to dig lugworm than catch fish, so wait until low water then go and collect some more bait. In Fenit town itself there is a pier from which some truly amazing catches have been made. Big common skate, tope, monkfish, undulate ray and conger are always on the cards, so make your tackle strong, and fish with a big side of mackerel for bait. You can of course use lugworm on the smaller hooks to entice the flounders, but I have found the crabs to be a nuisance, especially during the slack water period. Far better to fish on a big spring tide when more food and therefore bigger fish, will be on the move.

The boat fishing in the surrounding Tralee Bay is also legendary, and has long held top spot in the record listings for being the best producer of undulate rays. The area is very shallow, under 20 feet in many places, yet big common skate to over 100 lbs, monkfish over 60 lbs, tope over 40 lbs and a host of bull huss and dogfish are caught here by the charter boats each year. If you can take a boat to the deeper water outside the main body of land, and fish over the many pinnacle rocks that litter the bottom you will fill the boxes with pollock, codling, and conger eel. Plenty of blue sharks swim these waters offshore, but are seldom fished for as most anglers want to try their hand at the shallow water sport in the bay. The hotel at the base of Fenit pier is the place to enquire for a charter boat.

From the principal town of Tralee you can drive out onto the Dingle peninsula and the Ring of Kerry. But spare a day for Tralee itself, which has a racecourse, greyhound track and good golf course. The Festival of Kerry (International Rose of Tralee) is at the beginning of September, when, recalling the famous song, a rose of Tralee is chosen from girls of Irish descent from all over the world.

The only good boat fishing is to be had from Dingle harbour, but the entire length of this peninsula offers great shore fishing, the best of which starts at Castlegregory. Either side of this town is all surf fishing for bass and flatfish, the best of which come to lugworm baits fished on the bottom on a breezy day when the surf is 'up'. Further west at Kilshannig Point, Scraggane Bay and Fahamore the ground is rougher offering diverse sport with not only bass, but pollock, wrasse and coalfish. The town of Cloghane in the bowl of the legendary Brandon Bay has the most superb surf beaches in a strong westerly that you could imagine. Here on peeler crab or lugworm you have a good chance of a big bass, plaice or flounder in beautiful surroundings. Moving round to the south-west you have Brandon Creek where rock fishing on the eastern shore gives pollock, wrasse and conger. There is some good high water pier fishing for mullet and small strap conger which make for some fun fishing. At Smerwick Harbour in Ballydavid there is good mixed shore sport for the usual species. Other good points depending on the wind direction would be Ballyferriter, Dunquin and Ventry Harbour. The wrasse fishing at Slea Head which is a south-facing rock fishing platform is superb. I once heard of two anglers taking seventy wrasse here on crab and lugworm in just one session.

Finally, you couldn't mention the Dingle peninsula without mentioning Inch Strand. Long time favourite bass mark for hundreds of anglers, it is, alas, now a shadow of its former self due to the greed of overfishing. There are still bass present in enough numbers to make them a worthwhile fishing proposition, and indeed the scenery is breathtaking enough anyway, but this fine spot was once the best ever surf bass mark in the whole of Europe. Fish it once, just to say you've fished there! Tope still run there, and can be taken from the west facing strand on a large fillet of fresh mackerel cast out a long way. Lugworm can be dug from the mudflats behind the strand.

The boat fishing as far as charter fishing expeditions go is still relatively in its infancy. George Burgum operates the 36 foot *Skua* out of Dingle harbour and can offer some very good mixed fishing and is always willing to try an experiment or two in an effort to discover new grounds. Anchoring the boat in the very shallow water near Inch Strand can give sport with bull huss, spurdog packs, mackerel, rays and even tope, which seem to average around 30 lbs apiece in the late autumn. Off Slea Head George knows several rough ground marks and you can catch pollock, cod and mackerel, all into double figures. Outside the line of mainland in the deeper water there are plenty of blue sharks from June to October, and there seems every opportunity of taking the bigger porbeagle sharks that feed in the deep water close to shore,

Many have been sighted, and several tangled in commercial fishermen's nets, so hopefully in a year or two a complete new sportfishery may be opened up by George. Much of the water that George fishes is sheltered from any but the worst winds, so it is worth noting that if the wind is lifeless and the sea is flat then there will be no surf on the beaches to stir the bass. Therefore go out boat fishing. If the wind blows too much for the boat, the surf will be up and the bass chances high. Go shore fishing. This quick change of your plans will mean you are in an area that allows you to capitalise on each species, and enjoy County Kerry for what it is

Taken in August 1987, on the last day of a nine-day expedition to the west coast, the author landed a strange looking sunfish of 771lb 9oz. The port was Crookhaven, the boat the *Jan Steen* captained by Dutchman Hans (Bear) Havinga. This fish beat the old European record.

– one of the most productive all-round fishing areas, and certainly the cream of scenery as far the west coast of Ireland goes.

County Cork

Located back to the east from Kerry, the heartland of traditional Irish music, Cork is an area steeped in history. Wide farms with acres of golden grain, cattle on the lush hillsides, subtropical gardens and dark forests. A diverse topography, the basic geology of the county is carboniferous and red sandstone. This runs in an east-west fault that gives the county a series of ridges. The great rivers of Cork, the Bandon, and Lee, and the Blackwater flow from west to east along the valleys between the ridges, then make sudden right angle turns and make for the sea. Many minerals have been extracted from this county in the past. Coal, copper, lead, manganese, silver and even some traces of gold have been found. Cork is a sort of history of Ireland in miniature, and from each period there are places and monuments you can visit. People first came to Cork around 6000 B.C. Small worked flints are still picked up in ploughed fields dating from the remote past, and the 'kitchen middens' of oyster shells around the shores of Cork harbour may be of very ancient date, when people lived by hunting, fishing and gathering shell fish.

Various guided tours take place in and around Cork City, and the tourist will find plenty to do in the city centre itself. Cork City is the lifeline for tourism in the south being the first port of entry for most people. Many of the towns and villages along the tourist routes have their annual festivals, events and entertainments. The county is linked to other areas by a good network of rail from Cork City, and there is an airport as well. Two continental car ferries are at Ringaskiddy near the town centre, and CIE, Ireland's transport company, provide a good bus service to many parts of the county. Full details from CIE or any tourist information office. There are year round tourist information offices at Cork City, Tourist House, Grand Parade, tel: (021) 273251, and Skibbereen (028) 21766. Seasonal offices operate during the June to September period in the towns of Youghal, Fermoy, Cork Airport, Cork Ferryport, Kinsale, Clonakilty, Bantry and Glengarriff.

Cork airport is just 6km from the city centre, and the Aer

Lingus Ticket Office is at 38 Patrick St, tel: (021) 274331. The B & I line office is at 42 Grand Parade, tel: (021) 273024, and the Automobile Association is at 9, Bridge St, tel: (021) 505155.

Fishing in Cork

The best of the all-round fishing for boat and shore enthusiasts is at Courtmacsherry. Tucked into a sea filled valley, the Courtmacsherry Hotel has a picturesque view of both verdant hillsides and fish filled estuary. There is a large charter fleet of several fishing vessels, most of which are Tourist Board approved which is run by Marc Gannon, from the Deep Sea Angling centre on the pier. For the shore fisherman there are two very good species to try for. The mullet are not only numerous but big as well, and run up the estuary on a flood tide to seek out their food on the mudflats and creeks that run up to Timoleague. In this town there is, a bridge. And from this bridge you can cast your line for shoals of mullet that have the unsavoury habit of feeding in the blood from the slaughterhouse at Timoleague's butchers. At certain times of the day, an area at the base of this bridge actually runs a browny red, and the mullet are right there in the thick of it. An unsavoury place, but I can assure you when you see the size of the mullet as they cruise in the margins, it more than makes up for it. They can be taken on pieces of pork fat floatfished on a small hook. Groundbaiting is obviously not needed! At the pier in Courtmacsherry you can also catch the mullet at high water on pieces of mackerel, tiny pieces no larger than your little finger nail, floatfishing it close in to the kelp growing on the side of the pier. Also present and living in the cracks in the stonework at the bottom of the pier are the conger, and these are nearly always large fish over the double figure mark, and up to twenty pounds. The hotspot is right over the steps on the outside of the jetty, the best method being to leger using only a one ounce weight, a piece of mackerel or pollock fillet about six feet out from the wall. The optimum feeding time is critical. Half an hour either side of high water, and don't let them take too much line before you strike. They will simply disappear into the stonework and you will be forced to pull for a break. There is a bass mark on the opposite side of the estuary from a small jetty, but it is again only a high water mark as the tidal flow over the mudflats make it all but impossible to fish at other times. On the outside of the headlands you can take a wide variety of species from bass to flounders and wrasse. Some of the better marks are to the west of Courtmacsherry in the bay that leads out to the Old Head peninsula. Laherne Rocks fish best on the first two hours of flood tide for wrasse on the float. There is a danger of being cut off by the tide so take care in watching a flood tide, especially a big spring tide, which fills in quickly. Next to it is Garretstown Strand, which is adjacent to Laherne Rocks, but it does require a good surf to make the bass feed. The prettiest place of all is White Strand, which in a full gale produces a creaming surf that brings on the bass, especially if you can leger peeler crab.

For collecting bait for shore fishing, there are crab around the base of the pier in Courtmacsherry and other rock areas, and plenty of lugworm beds right in front of the Courtmacsherry Hotel, which makes digging them almost a pleasure before breakfast! The boats that operate from Courtmacsherry will specialise in fishing for the blue shark in an area of water drawn in a line from the Old Head and the Seven Heads. The further you can get out the better, and you will need a wind of force two to four to give you the best drifting conditions. On a good day you can expect up to ten shark runs in a full day although some may drop the mackerel baits. By fishing closer inshore and anchoring over the rough ground around the Old Head you can have great fun with the conger population, which although not large, are certainly numerous. Drifting will produce pollock and mackerel on the feathers. In Courtmacsherry Bay there are a few areas still largely unexplored where Mark Gannon believes the large common skate are. It may be worth a day at this, for they rarely come under the 100 lb mark.

Around the headland a few miles is the second of the top sharking ports in the south, Kinsale. Nestling between hillside and sea it is one of the most historic and picturesque towns in County Cork. A centre for yachting, sea angling, gourmet restaurants and golf, it has always had a sense of maritime adventure about it. The shore fishing is excellent for mullet, although you should pick either early morning or late evening to avoid the boat traffic of day. In the town, to the north side of the river Bandon is a mark known as Conger Hole. A flood tide here produces codling, conger, flounder, dogfish and even coalfish, which is unusual so far south. Sandy Cove, at the entrance to Kinsale harbour yields plenty of flatfish on lugworm, and dogfish on fish strip for those anglers putting out a long line to reach the sand flats.

More information on local shore fishing hotspots can be obtained by dropping in to the Trident Hotel and Angling Centre,

World's End, Kinsale, tel: (021) 772301. They can also give you the relevant information on the booking on the many tourist approved charter boats working out from there. Some of the top boats are as follows. *Enterprise* 38ft; *Trident Star* 36ft; *Kern* 34ft; *Raparee* 34ft; *Dromderrig* 34ft; *Moonlighter* 34ft; *Peggy G* 32ft; and finally the *Shamrock Gannett* 36ft.

Being just round the corner from Courtmacsherry, Kinsale boats are fishing similar grounds and therefore catch the same sort of species. If you get tired of walking the tourist routes in Cork City you can grab a day fishing here, for Barry Twomey runs the Crosshaven Sea Angling Centre, at Whispering Pines, Crosshaven and can assist with the use of two boats: the *'Norma T'* a 36ft craft, and the *Monica T*, a larger 52ft vessel, tel: (021) 831448. Being based in Cork Harbour he can also put you in touch with some of the better shore marks, but try the following anyway. Deepwater Quay at Cobh, has great fishing for conger, ray, codling, whiting, flounder and coalfish with crab, fishbait or mussel being the best baits. Further along to the west is Lynch's Quay which offers good autumn and winter fishing for codling, dabs and flounder. In summer it is mainly ray and dogfish. Round the coast to the east is Whitegate Bay which offers bottom fishing for bass and flounder. All round this huge natural harbour there are shore marks to be tried.

Indeed, virtually the whole of Ireland has a potential for rod and line sportfishing that may never be truly tapped. I hope that is so. Because more than half the excitement of fishing this country's coastline is that you never really know what you are going to come up with next. It's one of the last true adventure playgrounds of nature left as yet undamaged by man. Make the most of it now, for unlike the granite cliffs that gird Ireland's shores, it may not last for ever!

MADEIRA

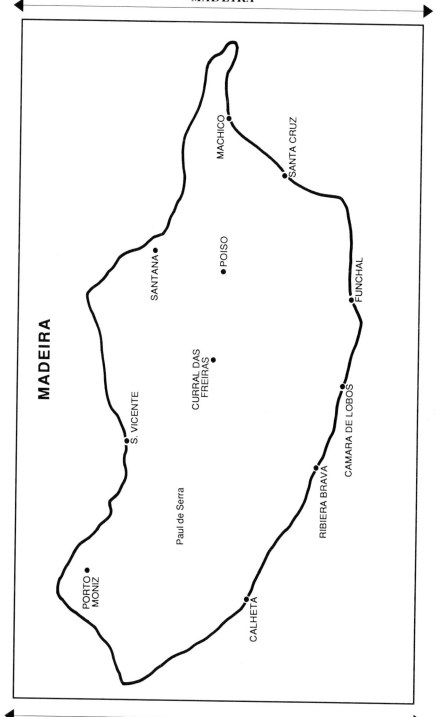

MADEIRA

Travel Tips

Access

Flying to the island of Madeira is usually via mainland Portugal, and invariably Lisbon. From here, depending on your particular carrier's timings, you can either connect direct for a flight to the island, or spend an overnight in a Lisbon hotel before making your connection the following day. Comparative distances as a guide to its location in the eastern Atlantic are as follows: 978km south-west of Lisbon, 545km from Cape Djouchi (Africa), and 443km from the island of Tenerife in the Canary Islands. The national carriers, TAP Air Portugal offer scheduled services, and can make connections via Lisbon for you. Air Europe also charter there, but it is a relatively simple matter to contact your local travel agent for either a package charter costing, or a routing through TAP Air Portugal. There is little point in mentioning the fact that some cruise liners stop off at the main harbour of Funchal, as this would be impractical for anybody wanting to get to the island quickly. Landing at the airport in itself is almost worth the journey, as the final approach is near the mountains and low over the sea!

Health

Madeira is owned by the Portuguese and there are no specialised regulations regarding health or immigration in force. No innoculations are compulsory, and the only entry requirement is a valid British passport. The weather is such that there is no likelihood of large numbers of mosquitoes, although it is always best to include a small personal first aid kit for the treatment of minor cuts, scratches and ailments. There are many chemists that can give you assistance in the capital of Funchal, any one of which can be found in the tourist guide information booklet supplied by the Portuguese Tourist Office. There is also one chemist on the island of Porto Santo. There are around eight hospitals and clinics on both Madeira and the other island of Porto Santo, but ensure you have adequate insurance cover before you leave Britain. This can usually be arranged through your local travel agent.

Ground Transportation

The island is well served by many taxis, available at the airport, tourist centres, or town and city taxi ranks. There are over fifteen listed in the tourist booklet for the centre of Funchal, two for Machico and two for the island of Porto Santo. If you want a cheaper mode of transport that also allows you to see the village way of life then try the bus service. Buses leave almost entirely from Funchal, travelling to different parts of the island and then returning to Funchal. The three main departure areas are Largo do Pelourinho, Avenida do Mar and Ruo do Consolheiro. They run through many places of interest mainly stopping at the following places: Assomada, Raposeira, Machico, Canical, Camacha, Corticeiras, Curral das Freiras, Cabo Girao, Camara de Lobos, Ponta da Oliveira, Boaventura, Sao Vicente, Ribeira Brava, Ponto do Sol, and Romeiras. If you really wish to go it entirely alone, then there are many hire car companies to choose from. The only requirement is a valid British driver's licence, and take your passport along as well in case they need that number too. In Funchal you have Atlas, Europcar, Hertz and Inter Rent to name but a few. From Machico there is an Inter Rent agency, and at the airport both Hertz and Rodavante supply cars. The taxis are all identified by the black and green livery.

Accommodation

There are many hotels smothering this delightful vocanic island, most rated on the 1–5 star basis, while the lower price range affords apartment hotels, motels, pensions and self-catering. In accordance with international practice, on registering at any hotel the guest must state how long he intends to stay, and the occupation of that accommodation ends at approximately midday. This may alter from hotel to hotel, but is a good general guide. The price of a room generally includes a continental breakfast, and/or lunch and dinner. The charter companies generally include breakfast and dinner in their room prices. There is little problem in taking a light lunch as Madeira is famous for its choice of bars, tea rooms and restaurants, and for these it is simply a matter of walking around and choosing your own. Should you wish to eat out in the evening I can honestly say it is well worth trying the local fish restaurants as an island generally has an extensive commercial fishing industry and thereby constant supply of fresh fish. In Funchal you should try *Gavina's* restaurant on the ocean front, where the scabbard fish known locally as espada, is first class. Try also the squid, octopus and espadarte, or swordfish. Washed down with one of the many local wines there is no finer way to spend a lunchtime.

Part of the magic of Madeira lies not only in the exciting deep sea fishing it offers, but in the idyllic pace of life in both the remote villages, or even the main Avenida seen here in the capital, Funchal.

The Island

The entire Madeira archipelago consists of three islands: the main island of Madeira, the Desertas and Porto Santo. They are situated in the North Atlantic about an hour's flight north of the Canary Islands. Madeira derived its name from the dense forests which once covered the island in lush green vegetation. The climate is conservative all year round, tempered by the surrounding ocean, the thermal range seldom exceeding 7°C. According to legend the island was discovered by an Englishman and his mistress who became shipwrecked there in 1346. Later, in 1419, Zarco claimed the islands on behalf of Henry the Navigator. In the early years of sailing ships, the island became an important stepping stone for the loading and unloading of goods. Many ships from the east stopped here, and consequently the tropical and sub-tropical plants you see growing were brought by the different cultures.

Madeira is some 14 miles wide and 36 miles long, while the island of Porto Santo in the north-east is 9 miles by 3. The islanders had a flourishing trade in the famous Madeira wines grown on the lush mountain slopes. The sweetest is Malmsey, less sweet is Bual, Verdelho is medium and Sercial is the driest. By the middle of the 18th century, the wines of Madeira were favourites of the Royal Courts of Europe and were also enjoyed in America. But in 1852 the vines were devastated by a form of mildew called Oidium Tuckeri. Within ten years shipments fell to less than a tenth of their previous average. Experiments found that vines could be treated with sulphur, and it took until 1861 for the vines to regain full health. A second scourge attacked them in 1872 in the form of a louse, and it was discovered that American vines grafted on to the exsisting stock were immune to this pest.

Dated Madeiras are unblended wines that are aged for at least ten years in the Madeira Wine Company lodges before being bottled. It has an amazing longevity and can still be fine, sound and drinkable when as old as 150 years. Wickerwork, flower growing and lace making are among the local industries well worth seeing. If you have the time visit some of the areas renowned for embroidery, tapestry, jewellery and leather goods. Of the places to see, the fish and vegetable market in the centre of Funchal is worth a visit, to drink in the heady smells and colours.

The Orchid House and Botanical Garden and the Madeira Wine Lodges are all good interest points.

Along the coast there is Camara de Lobos, a fishing village virtually the same as when Sir Winston Churchill painted there. Camacha, after a day spent driving through the mountains, is the centre of the wickerwork industry, while Cabo Girao boasts the world's second highest sea cliff. At Santana you can see the typical thatched houses with pointed roofs, and at Ponta Moniz you can swim in the volcanic rock sea pools. The mountain drives, whether by taxi or by hire car are a refreshing change from a day on the ocean chasing the fish, and you can stop at some of the local spots for a caldeirada (fish soup),or bolo de mel, the local Maderia honey cake. Or if the pangs of hunger strike really deep try the beef on the spit, or espetada as it is known. While in the mountains you can stop at the local trout farm and see just how many fish can be artificially fed in the stock ponds. For a small licence fee you can also fish for them in the mountain streams and pools. On one of my many excursions into this area I armed myself with a flyrod and set about stalking some of the rainbows in the deep, clear rock pools. They were very hard to get near, let alone present a fly to, and it was only later at lunch time that my taxi driver informed me a match held the previous day was won with sweetcorn on the hook! He could see no point in my using an artificial fly, and offered to buy me a tin from the local grocer's. I declined, determined to extract one of the stream's occupants on traditional methods. Indeed I did so, landing several small rainbows on a yellow baby doll fly, the nearest colour I had to sweet corn! While up there in the cool atmosphere of eucalyptus and clouds you can walk the levadas. These are old irrigation channels cut through the woodland and are even coded according to the walker's capability on a rating from 1 for beginners to 4 for experienced climbers.

An ideal one day tour would be to depart in the morning from Funchal to the west and the tiny fishing village of Camara de lobos. With its colourful splash of roof, boats and sky it is easy to see why Churchill often painted here. From here you can drive up to one of the highest points at Curral das Freiras, then return down the same route to Funchal and take lunch of squid, bread and a white wine at Gavina's restaurant. In the afternoon drive through Monte and Poiso from where you can get a splendid view of Funchal laid out below you. Continue up the road to Ariero, then back across to Ribeiro Frio and down again to Funchal, not forgetting to sample some of the honey cake on the way! There is a restaurant at Poiso, and it is a good place to try espetada. At night harbour and street lights flicker on and the whole of Funchal takes on a fairyland twinkling.

For entertainment there is the Casino da Madeira, and most of the hotels will provide their own entertainment. There are also local bars and discotheques available. Voltage is usually 220v with facilities for a continental two pin plug. If you have hair driers, shavers etc, why not buy one of those multi-adaptor plugs at the duty free airport? The banks are open weekdays 08.30–11.45

The islands main claim to fame must be in the production of its wines, especially the four types of Madeira. The clarity in this 1863 Vintage Boal makes a trip out fishing even more difficult once it has been tasted!

and again 13.00–14.45. The unit of currency is the escudo, which is divided into 100 parts called centavos, and a $ type sign is used to divide the two. Most of the hotels also have exchange facilities.

Again, if you have a day you wish to spend shore touring, then try the island of Porto Santo. It is attractive, with both a long sandy beach, and a rugged coastline. The rocks offer good potential for bluefish and many of the sea bream and mullet take on a floatfished fish strip bait. The island is only 25 miles from Madeira but it has six miles of long sandy beach stretching along its south coast. Vila Baleria is its tiny capital, where you can see the house where Christopher Columbus once lived. Accommodation here is limited and advance booking is necessary, but the day trip alone is worth while as there are several restaurants and bars. Travel to Porto Santo from Madeira is either by boat (three hours or less) or by plane (fifteen minutes). For the beach enthusiast Madeira is disappointing as it is almost entirely volcanic cliffs dropping straight into the Atlantic Ocean. However, there is a magnificent new lido complex on the ocean front in Funchal and here facilities are excellent for the family to get a suntan in safety while enjoying the swimming and food as well. Fortunately much of Madeira has retained that air of yesteryear. Its people are quiet and hospitable, and the colours and countryside of that lush green terraced agriculture is as unchanged now as it was fifty years ago. Commercialism often brings revenue to an island, but if it is at the expense of a unique culture I feel it may be too high a price to pay. For the time being though it remains a great place to visit for a fishing holiday.

The Fishing

For the shore fisherman, the entire coastline of Madeira offers an almost untapped potential for a wide variety of reef fish. The larger predators, shark, billfish and the tuna are to be caught out to sea where the bottom contours drop away quickly to tremendous depths. Having said that, on rare occasions the massive big eye tuna shoals for which the island is famous, often run extremely close in to the shoreline. In fact of all the places I have visited in the world, Madeira is the place where they run in closest. The commercial tuna fishery consists of large boats manned by many men who catch massive tuna using just a strengthened bamboo pole. No reel, no fighting chair, no fast boat to back down on the fish. The tuna shoal, once located, is brought near to the boat by a hosepipe sprayed on to the surface of the sea, both to mask the hull of the boat from the fish beneath, and to simulate a shoal of frightened food fish scattering on the surface. Small livebaits, usually sardines, are kept in livebait tanks and thrown overboard after being disabled so they spiral near the surface. The big tuna smash into these greedily, and of course every so often they take a livebait that is attached to the hook and bamboo pole of the fisherman. He strikes, and in that split second the tuna must be hauled aboard, for if he gets his head down, those powerful thrusts of the tail will simply snap the line. Some years ago the local tuna fishermen from Funchal saw birds diving just a half mile from the harbour. They gathered their equipment and raced out to see a huge shoal of tuna only 700 yards away. Being professional fishermen they took full advantage of the situation and after just 35 minutes they had caught 28 tuna averaging 150 lbs! So of course there is that opportunity of a big fish roving near the shoreline, but I think you can safely discount landing a 150 lb bigeye tuna on a shore rod!

With such deep water close in the angler can either fish with spinners and flashing spoon for species like the bluefish and European barracuda. The water is very clear and if at all possible a livebait suspended under a float should be used in preference to the lures. The best casting spoons are made by Ryobi and are called the Odin. The one ounce class when fished with 8 lb line and a spinning rod will cast like a bullet and can sink quite quickly through the water. Never start the retrieve as soon as the lure hits the water, far better to let it flutter down thirty feet then start it back towards you. Most of the takes will come as you are ready to lift the spoon from the water. With deep water close in, any small fish stay within a few yards of the rocks and underwater caves as a sort of sanctuary from any predators. Of course the predators know this and often search in close to the rocks, especially during the poorer light conditions of early morning and late evening.

In the harbour of Funchal there is a good depth of water, and this is well worth searching out with the aid of a pair of polaroids and long peaked hat. Often you can spot a school of mullet or some of the bream species cruising near the edge. The mullet shoals can be quite enormous, and can either be taken on bread paste, or with a small piece of shrimp bait. Early morning is the best time to fish for them, just after first light. Start by throwing some bread out on the surface to see if they will take it, and use a piece of crust and either a bubble float filled with water, or a piece of 'Floatbait' as a casting aid. If groundbaiting, a mixture of bread (locally bought rolls are fine) some bran and a few drops of pilchard oil. This is enhanced if you can get a few sardines from the market and crush them up in the mixture. Add water, and mash up, throwing in just a small amount to see what will rise in the water to feed on it. On the hook you can use either a piece of breadflake pinched on the hook, a piece of prawn or shrimp, or a piece of sardine. Use a float like a balsa bodied avon that takes a couple or three lead swan shot. About three feet would be the average depth to set the float, but if you want to try for the bream and snappers, you need to fish from the many rocky outcrops around the island, and use the same groundbait mixture as for the mullet, but set the float a lot deeper, around nine or ten feet. The hookbait should be a small piece of fresh fish, like mackerel or tuna (bonito) as this stays on the hook better in the swells that wash around the rocks. Squid and octopus can be purchased from the local fish market in Funchal and this represents probably the toughest strip bait to use when fishing from the rocks. I have also used it successfully in long narrow strips of four or five inches, attaching it to the treble hooks of my lure. This adds the attraction both for smell and visual, and is a tip worth using on any of the Atlantic islands when rock fishing.

As with the Canary Isles, I feel the harbour of Funchal, and to a lesser extent those of the smaller fishing villages, may well be worth a session or two for really big fish like stone bass and stingray that must surely frequent the shoreline littoral zone where most of the food is. Perhaps a night session with a large fillet of bonito cast well out on a running leger rig would give you a fish or two. In the east of the island the places I would suggest trying are around Ponta De S. Lourenco, and the harbour at Machico. In the south you have the excellent fishing around Funchal harbour, with rock platforms to the west at Camara de Lobos. Another area is to be found at Ponta do Sol and Calheta, while in the north-east a session at Porto Moniz can be productive. All along the north coast access down to sea level can be difficult, if not impossible. In fact great care should be exercised anywhere around the rocky coastline. Particular attention should be paid to the Atlantic swell on a rough sea, which sweeping across an open expanse as it does, can rise up ten feet even from a flat sea, so try to fish from rocks that are several feet above the waterline. It also may be best to go with another angler for safety, although the harbour at Funchal is both a good fishing area, and comfortable to fish from.

Most of the taxi drivers can be organised into dropping you off and collecting you at predetermined times, but if you have a hire car, then you are free to go where you please and stay as long as you like. The island of Madeira has yet to realise its full potential for deep sea fishing. The surrounding ocean is vast, and the surviving charter fleet for deep sea fishing is limited to just a few boats. They cater mainly for the tourist angler, and occasionally go out specifically after big marlin and tuna. The volcanic origin of the islands means that from the ocean floor, a great mountain burst up to form Madeira. The surrounding water is very deep, especially close to shore when compared to anywhere around the British coastline To give you an indication of the sort of depths that you have close to shore, around two miles out it can drop to 550 metres, while ten miles out you have 1500 metres. This allows the large pelagic predators to move in close to shore, but like the Canary Islands, there are no banks or shoals to hold the baitfish for any length of time. Everything is migrating past, and it depends entirely on the fish whether they decide to come in close past the island, or stay 150 miles offshore. However, there is always the chance of catching something close in, and trolling slowly with deep swimming rapala lures can give you a large grouper, barracuda or specimen bluefish. It is a method that could be tried from a small commercial open boat rather than the more expensive gameboat. The bluefish in particular run to a very good size for the species, and can top 20 lbs, possibly even taking a world record, but even though they are prized as a sporting fish in America, they are often neglected by the tourist and locals alike.

There are some localised hotspots and these are exploited by the gameboat captain who should be trolling your fishing lures in all the best spots. About twenty miles off the port of Funchal lies the Desertas Islands. Again of a volcanic nature, they rise up from the ocean floor and make a fine holding area for both reef and bait fish. The predators are of course never very far away, and so these islands are good for marlin, shark and tuna. The shark are caught by drifting with the current and wind, and breaking up small sardines to attract them with an oily smell trail. A baited hook of either a bunch of sardines or a bonito are then fished away from the boat. Although tuna can be taken from a drifting boat by chumming and live or deadbait fishing, it is a method not practised in Madeira. They troll with either artificial lures, large konaheads for the marlin, and smaller weighted plastic squids for the tuna, or with a deadbait. Occasionally if a live fish can be caught that too is rigged and fished live, possibly the best method of getting a take from a shark or marlin. For lure colours the local fishermen favour red and green, or blue and white, although I have yet to fish the area using high tech lures like the 'Tornado', and 'Doorknob' lures from America that can be so effective when trolled at high speed.

Fishing at higher boat speeds means that you cover a lot more ground during the course of the day, and therefore stand more chance of making a hookup with a fish. While the shark will not be fast enough to catch a fast trolled lure, a marlin or tuna will have no difficulty at all in catching one. Of course much depends on the owner of the charter vessel, who may not wish to convert the extra cost of fuel spent into a good fish in the boat. Things are always slow to change in fishing circles, and islanders anywhere in the world are the slowest to make any sort of change or adaptation. While the wind can come from any quarter, the big tuna shoals seem to bite better during a north-easterly blow. The sea temperature can also play a very decisive part in the production of big game fish. The coastline water is often influenced by the Canaries' current and in the months from July right up to October, can reach a good level. Generally speaking, the warmer the water, the better the fishing. During this period it can average out somewhere between 20° and 25°C .

As well as the Desertas, other marks that are used by the boat captains as productive areas are Barlavento to the east, plus several other marks close to shore from Ponta da Pargo in the west, and back to Funchal in the south. In the north-east, if you have no wind and are able to take the boat there, you can fish off Porto Minic, which is a good area for wahoo. The south is the most popular area for the boats to work, mainly because of the proximity of Funchal harbour, but once several miles south from the port, they work areas between Quinte Grande, Ponta do Sol, Madalena do Mar and Jardim do Mar. The wahoo can be taken only a mile or so from shore and can run to a very good weight, occasionally topping the 80 lb mark. Should you be fortunate enough to catch one try to get your hotel chef to grill a steak or two. They really do present fine eating.

While it may be possible to negotiate with a local fisherman for a smallboat to take you inshore trolling or bottom fishing there is really only one main charter boat operation. This is called *Turipesca* and is run by Euginia Braz with two or three boats. One is a 40 foot Chris Craft called the *Briso-do-Mar*. This is powered by two Volvo 124 h p diesel engines and is fully equipped with fighting chair, basic tackle and outriggers. The *Maribella* is the second boat, a 37 foot cruiser equipped with two Perkins 115 h p engines, and fitted with fighting chair, outriggers and basic tackle. There is also a third available. The 55 foot *Flora da Gibalta* is a commercial fishing boat fitted with two fighting chairs, but is much slower as it is powered by a single 165 h p Cummins diesel. This latter boat would be better suited for slow trolling with livebaits, or drifting for sharks. As yet, a fully equipped modern American style big game boat has yet to make an impact on Madeiran big game fishing, but I feel it is sure to come sooner or later, because the potential for the big four species, tuna, marlin, swordfish and shark, really is incredible.

As an indication of the massive sizes attained by predator species in these rich waters it is best to look at the statistics attained by the professional fleet operating there. These may be the long distance tuna boats that fish with water spray, livebait and the bamboo poles. Or they may be the single man small boats that launch off tiny coves and beaches, fishing the deep water reefs with a handline from a drifting boat. Or they may be one of the thriving commercial night fleets, that stay out during the hours of darkness to catch the deep swimming scabbard fish, or espada as it is known. Ungainly, long and ugly fish, but beautiful to eat, they are taken on baited handlines in colossal depths of water. By fishing at night, these same fishermen catch the big broadbill swordfish, so highly prized by game fishermen, and through their catches we can see there are indeed clearly defined taking periods for this sought after species. During the daytime they bite best in the months from February to April, at a distance from the coastline of around two miles. For night fishing different months have been found to be successful for them. Fishing at a distance of nearly ten miles from the coast, over the 1500 metre depth mark, they are taken in the months of July to September. By taking into account these areas and depths as well as times of the year, the enterprising angler can put himself in the best possible position to make contact with the species he seeks. In the case of the broadbill swordfish, I would advise the use of a deep fished livebait like a ray's bream, dropped down from a drifting boat at the distances mentioned above. From the point of view of catching a big marlin, there can be few places in the north Atlantic that offer, quite literally, the potential of an all-tackle world record. In 1985 a blue marlin was weighed in at the commercial station in Funchal and

In July 1987 came the new marlin record for Madeira, even as the author's ink was drying on the paper, with his own opinion that the island's true potential for big fish had yet to be exploited. This monster Atlantic blue marlin tipped the scales at a massive 1,210 lbs, and was taken aboard the Briso do Mar, one of the Turipesca fleet, mentioned by the author.

it tipped the scales at 1540 lbs. This came from the area south-west of the Desertas, and was followed in 1986 by yet another blue marlin that weighed 1320 lbs. Commercial fishermen have also accounted for mako shark to nearly 1000 lbs, bluefin tuna to 946 lbs and the bigeye tuna to 396 lbs.

Of course you cannot really equate commercial statistics to a rod and line charter boat operation, but nevertheless it does give an indication of the weights possible from some of the sporting species. In 1980 the largest blue marlin on rod and line weighed 990 lbs, and one that was lost during a long fight was estimated to weigh 1300 lbs. Apparently it fought for five hours before breaking loose. In 1984 two of the bigger blue marlin weighed 704 lbs and 792 lbs, and some rare spearfish were caught. 1985 was an excellent year for the bigeye tuna, but the marlin failed to show in any sort of numbers. This illustrates how different each season can be at a deep water venue, and how it is almost totally dependent on the migratory patterns of the pelagic fish. 1986 saw the marlin back again with a 550 pounder landed, then a near 800 pounder and another nearing 700 lbs, when a tourist angler fought the fish for two hours before deciding he had enough punishment and walked away from the rod! That's what they call beginner's luck, and that man will never really know how lucky he was to hook a fish that size. The spearfish showed up in quantity, ranging from 60 lbs to over 80 lbs, and seemed to coincide with an increase in the number of spearfish being caught in the same year from the island of Gran Canaria, in the Canary Islands. Many of the charter boat's anglers are simply tourists who fancy a day out at sea to catch a big fish. They have no prior knowledge of just how hard the fight may be with a marlin or bluefin tuna, and often break off a fish that a more experienced angler could have landed. On the other hand, many boat captains say they would rather have an enthusiastic beginner on a big fish than an experienced fisherman. The reasoning behind this being that the beginner will do what he is told in coping with a big fish, but of course the experienced angler tends to think he knows it all. While the island of Madeira offers the holiday angler some good shore and boat fishing, he must remember that as soon as he puts his lure or bait into the water there is a chance, albeit very small, that an extremely large marlin, tuna or shark may just come along. The fight is more likely to be measured in hours rather than minutes, so be prepared. More likely both you and your family will enjoy a pleasant day trolling in the bluewater, maybe catching the odd fish or two as a bonus. But Madeira also has big species, which is why I recommend it as one of the best places in Europe to try!

While your local travel agent should be able to set up the actual holiday package for you, it may be worth booking the gameboats in advance, especially if you have no wish to pay the full charter price yourself, and only want to share with other people of a like mind. This is known as a split charter, but it is essential to let the charter boat know well in advance to allow them time to organise their booking schedule. You can do this by writing to *Turipesca*, Euginia Braz, Madeira Gamefishing Centre, Marinha do Funchal, Madeira, tel: 3-10-63, or 4-24-68, telex 72221 Braz. P. Their office is located right by the marina on the Avenida do Mar, and is a kiosk with boards of fishing photos outside. If you require further information on booking hotels, car hire and so on yourself the local tourist office will be delighted to assist, and can supply you with information guides, maps and brochures. Contact Direccao Regional do Turismo, Avenida Arriaga 18,9000 Funchal, Madeira, Portugal, tel: 29-057, telex 72 DTM FNCP. If in England, you can contact the Portuguese National Tourist Office, Miss Ferreira, New Bond Street House, 1/5, New Bond Street, London. WIY ONP. They will also be able to supply you with much information and literature on the island.

PORTUGAL

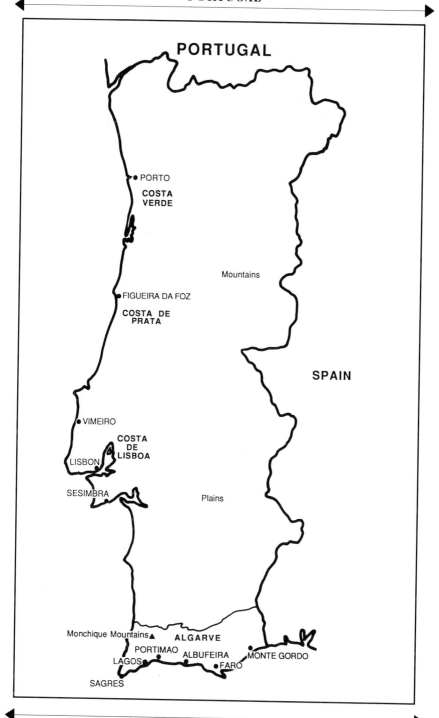

Travel Tips

Access

The benefit of travelling to this colourful country is that you can walk into your local travel agent and simply either book a complete package holiday to any one of the tourist centres, or book a flight and drive your way round, stopping wherever your fancy takes you. Many people, especially fishermen, prefer the freedom offered by simply booking a flight and picking up a hire car to drive either up to the mountains or down to the coast. However, please remember that during peak seasons in the coastal regions hotels are often overbooked, so always have a second venue up your sleeve just in case you have to make alternative plans. Aside from any of a multitude of package holidays, which do really offer the best value for money, the scheduled air services of the national carrier TAP Air Portugal are as follows:

London (Heathrow) – Lisbon: TAP-Air Portugal and British Airways.
London (Gatwick) – Lisbon: British Airways and Danair Services.
London (Heathrow) – Oporto: TAP - Air Portugal.
London (Gatwick) – Oporto: British Airways.
London (Heathrow) – Faro: TAP-Air Portugal.
London (Gatwick) – Faro: British Airways.
Birmingham – Faro: British Airways.

Various tariffs are in operation for all destinations including Apex and Saver fares. For details of fares and reservations, please contact the airline concerned, or book through your local travel agent.

TAP-Air Portugal: reservations 01-828-0262, fares -01-839-1031.
British Airways (or branches): 01-897-4000.
Danair Services: 01-680-1011.

For charter flights without taking the complete package holiday as well, it is best to look through the national daily newspapers. As for immigration requirements, no visas are required for holders of British passports, for visits of up to 60 days. A work permit is required for anyone wishing to work in Portugal.

Health

As always it is essential to ensure you have adequate insurance cover for any eventualities that may occur. This can be arranged for a nominal fee through your travel agent. No vaccinations are required for visitors from the UK unless there is an epidemic of any sort in the UK. An International Certificate of Vaccination is, however, required if you have travelled through a country with an epidemic, such as cholera, smallpox or yellow fever. There are many English speaking practitioners in Portugal , and there is a British hospital at 49, Rua Saraiva de Carvalho, Lisbon, tel: 602020. It is forbidden to take fresh meat into Portugal, but the standard duty-free items can be imported.

Money

The currency is the escudo, composed of 100 centavos. There is, at present, no limit to the amount of foreign currency, whether cash or travellers cheques, that may be taken into the country by visitors. On leaving the country, no more than 50,000 escudos per person in local currency and/or travellers cheques may be taken out. Money and travellers cheques may be changed at banks and hotels. Banking hours are from 08.30–11.45 and 13.30–14.45 Monday to Friday. In Lisbon, certain central branches are also open 18.00–23.00. In the Algarve the bank at the Vilamoura marina shopping centre is open daily from 09.00-21.00.

Ground Transportation

By train, there is a daily service in all the major cities, and 'sleeper' vans/carriages can be taken from Victoria (UK) to Paris then down to Portugal. But to get there more quickly and start fishing, use air routes if at all possible. There is an excellent national network of trains in Portugal, fares are cheap and it is a good way to see some of the countryside. Full particulars from mainline stations in Portugal. Portuguese railway time tables may be obtained from BAS overseas publications, 48–50 Sheen Lane, London SW14. In the summer months there is a motor-rail service Oporto/Lisbon/Faro, plus comfortable coach services which also cover the country (timetables are available from local tourist offices). The black and green taxis can be hired in the cities, towns and larger villages.

For the hire car driver, and this is how most fishermen will want to move around, there are the international road signs to watch. The speed limit in built up areas is 37 m p h, cars outside towns 55 m p h and motorways 75 m p h. The rental for most hire cars is on a daily basis plus a mileage charge, or on a weekly basis with unlimited mileage. The minimum age is 23 years for people who have held a full driving licence for at least one year. A British driving licence is valid and full insurance can be obtained on payment of a small supplement per day. It may be for

The bustling commercial port of Portimao often sees the unloading of the sardine boats after they have spent a night at sea. Here also, the mullet shoals are prolific.

The Country

Located at the south-west corner of Europe, Portugal offers not just good shore fishing potential, but sport in freshwater fishing as well. There are hundreds of miles of unspoilt rivers which make their way through both interesting and spectacular scenery. They are stocked and produce salmon, shad, black bass, trout, carp and barbel. With a near perfect climate it is often worth a drive out and a day away from the sea on the freshwater lakes and rivers really is refreshing. The capital, Lisbon, is known as the gateway to Europe, a bustling city that is culturally interesting for the tourist, but of little interest to the fisherman. He will want to get away to the many unspoilt beaches and rock marks to fish in the peace and solitude for which this country is so famous. The accommodation choice in the entire country is vast. A blending of both old and new, from a luxurious five star de luxe establishment to the network of pousadas (government inns), or a self-catering apartment down on the sun soaked Algarve coast.

Although diverse in topography you can best describe the country as having two sectors. The mountains in the north, giving way to the plains in the south. The sea flanks the entire west coast, running north to south you have the Costa Verde, Costa de Prata, Estoril, Lisbon and the Algarve. For the shore fisherman this represents some 600 miles of explorable coastline with over 200 species of fish, the specialities being grey mullet, bluefish, bass, bream and tope. From the boats you can try for several species of shark, the rare broadbill swordfish, tuna, rays or snapper. While there are a few charter boats available in the south along the Algarve, I would venture the suggestion that this west coast offers some exciting potential, should some enterprising businessman ever start a charter boat company there. The water is deep, straight out into the Atlantic, which is why the rocks and coves produce such good bass fishing. Wherever you choose to fish, it may be beneficial to contact one of the local fishing clubs, there are around 40 in all, and they should be able to put you in the better places for shore work. If a small fishing village really takes your fancy, why not see if you can get one of the local fishermen to take you out bottom fishing. They may be glad of the extra revenue and of course will know the surrounding seabed like the back of their hand. The more interesting sport comes down along the Algarve coast in the south, and it is here that most will want to take their family. There are tourist centres of course, where the beaches are packed in the summer months, but those same areas also have some massive shoals of mullet for the light tackle fisherman to try his hand at. In Portimao and Vilamoura you have commercial fishing operations where bigger boats moor up, offloading a colourful mixture of reef fish, squid and sardines. Some spillage is bound to occur and naturally the mullet shoals take full advantage of this. Look out too for the sewage outflows, for although unsavoury, they are the places where the grey mullet shoal up. The fish will be from half a pound up to four pounds, and occasionally larger.

Fishing is best done in the casual fashion. Have a few hours in the morning, then take a lunch of ham, cheese and local wine under the shade of a parasol by a café. Surely the most civilised thing to do in the heat of the day? Then fish again during the afternoon, by which time if you haven't caught a fish it doesn't really matter anyway, the wine still tasted good! The weather

The sewer outflows, although unsightly places to fish, are where the biggest shoals of mullet congregate. The local fishermen prefer to use a piece of mullet gut for bait, although bread paste spiced up with a little fish paste works as well.

An indication on how many mullet are along the Algarve coast is shown here by Christine Kent from Birmingham, who spent a week touring and fishing with her husband.

should be fine, as the Algarve averages some 3300 hours of sunshine every year, which is often more than many of the Med resorts. From Faro airport area all along the coast to the west you will find golden beaches, from which it is best to night fish with a sardine or similar fish bait legered on the bottom. That is when the snappers, bream and small stingray move in closer to shore, and of course you don't have all the watersports going on at that time. The better rock fishing will come at the western tip, at a place called Sagres. Here there used to be an excellent boatman who caught big sharks, but unfortunately he has died and nobody has replaced him. It is the home of the lobster fishing industry, and the town is where Prince Henry established his famous School of Navigation. The cliffs are impressive and you will be amazed to see the local shore fishermen casting out with 16 foot telescopic rods and fixed spool reels to catch the many reef fish below. A rugged beauty that needs some care when fishing as the cliffs really are sheer. The last time I boat fished there was from a yacht and I recall having several huge squid coming up to grab at my baits, eerie creatures that would undoubtedly have tasted better in a frying pan with peppers, than they looked in the water! There are also some big shoals of grey mullet present around the cliffs, though it is almost impossible to get down to them.

Portugal is situated very close to the continental shelf, where depths have been recorded of 3250 fathoms, or just under 20,000 feet! There is a platform running from the coast between fifty and one hundred miles wide where the depth is much less, ranging between 50 and 300 fathoms. Therefore the potential for some of the ocean's big predators to come up into this shallower water is great indeed. In the deep water are the scabbard fish, or espada, so prized as table fare. Each season the huge bluefin tuna pass close to shore on their journey into the Mediterranean, and up into the Aegean Sea, vast monsters of the tuna family that grow in excess of 1000 lbs. From the mainland the western port of Sesimbra used to boast some quite reasonable fishing for swordfish. Very good fish were caught, small dinghies being used as the fishing craft, while a larger support vessel is held in safety. The idea was to set a deep bait from a drifting boat, this was usually a live ray's bream, until a swordfish grabbed it. The fight from such small craft was exciting indeed. The swordfish still hunts in these waters, but alas nobody seems to offer the visiting angler a chance to fish for them. Sagres and Cape St. Vincent would be excellent places from which to try this, and you have the bonus of a shark or two. The shark fishing here used to be very good for big blue sharks in excess of 200 lbs. These were females that came in to drop their young, as the area is rich in baitfish like sardines and mackerel.

Along the coast at Portimao and Vilamoura there are a few charter boats operating trips, but they are geared mostly towards the tourist, and while it is certainly worth a day or two out with them, I wouldn't say the catches were too fantastic. I was told on the first trip I had there that there were plenty of blue sharks to be caught, so like many I envisaged several fish over the 200 lbs mark. Imagine my surprise when we landed about half a dozen blue sharks, and they were about 5 lbs apiece! Having said that they do occasionally pick up the odd mako shark around the 100 lb mark, and for that reason alone it is worth a trip. Let's face it, the weather is generally good and a trip out is enjoyable itself. Beware of the 'packed lunch included' rip-off. Better to take out your own food and a bottle of local rosé, that way you know you are going to enjoy it. The bottom fishing can be varied, but again the better fishing is way down west off Sagres, which of course is generally too far for the tourist boats to run.

Should you be able to charter a local commercial boat however, you could strike lucky with some very big reef fish. They have some of the species we get in the UK but they invariably run a lot larger. The tope for instance are said to reach 110 lbs, the stone bass, living near rocks and caves can top 60 lbs. The bluefish run over 12 lbs, rays over 40 lbs and the corvina or white bass as much as 90 lbs. This latter species can often be taken from rock fishing platforms where there is a good surf running. The swordfish reach an enormous size, certainly over 550 lbs and perhaps bigger. There are no hotspots as such, it really is just a question of finding a small commercial fishing boat, usually called a *peniche*. These are suitable for about four people to go bottom fishing, although if you strike a good bargain you might wish to take it yourself with just your family.

As a general guide to seasons, the climate is generally mild and stable. The dry season is between May and October when the average air temperature is around 75°F. The temperature of the water varies little between 60° and 65°F. Winds are generally light and blow off the mountains from the north, but during the month of August it can blow a bit. The mackerel arrive in June and stay till October, which is also prime time for blue shark, swordfish and the tuna. Should anybody start up specialised fishing for the swordfish, commercial catch statistics bear out the fact that September until November is the best time. This coincides with the island of Madeira, and of course the Azores islands, where there is a considerable commercial fishery. In both Sesimbra and Sagres it is worth visiting the local fish auctions to not only give you an unforgettable experience, but to let you see the type and size of different species there are to be encountered. Should you spend a day at somewhere on the Algarve coast, and the Luz Bay Club area is as good as any for apartments and villas, do make the most of the local seafood restaurants. The Portuguese are adept fishermen and their chefs first class in cooking fish. Local wines are both cheap and good to drink. If you hire a car, don't forget to spend a day up in the Monchique mountains, an ancient spa resort, with a market and picturesque 17th-century architecture. High in that clear mountain atmosphere there are local bars and restaurants, mingling with the eucalyptus trees. Try the starter of parma ham and melon with port. Main course of chicken piri-piri, and the strawberries and cream for dessert. The waiter can recommend the wine of the day, and I am sure you will find the weather, food and hospitality of the Portuguese people more than making up for any inadequacies in the fishing! If in the UK you can get leaflets and information from the Portuguese National Tourist Office, New Bond Street House, 1-5 New Bond Street, London. WIY ONP, tel: 01-493-3873. For enquiries about booking a boat from Vilamoura or Portimao on the Algarve coast, write to Rudolph Streur, Cepemar, Centro de Pesca Desportiva no Mar, Lda, Praca da Republica, 24-A, 8500 Portimao, Algarve, Portugal.

The seagulls whirl as they follow a sardine boat out from Lagos on its journey to the fishing grounds. The area is a nursery for small blue sharks, although occasionally small mako or bigger blues to 150 lbs can turn up.

FISHING TACKLE SUGGESTIONS

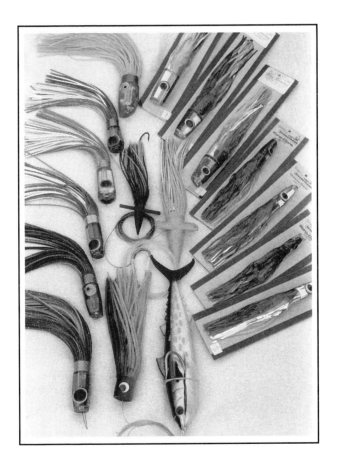

Fishing Tackle Suggestions

Rather than list the same items of tackle for every single country section, I thought it better to include a list of suitable tackle and equipment, together with some suggestions for travelling abroad, in a separate section. Every angler has his own favourite rod, reel and line, and of course most of the charter boat operations listed have a supply of tackle for the fisherman within their charter price. While it is probably sufficient for the general tourist, I feel it best to let the reader know exactly what I advise as usage for these countries.

Invariably the charter boats will have no light tackle, that is to say anything less than 30 lb class gear. When shore fishing I know of nowhere in any of the countries concerned where you can hire tackle at all. Tackle shops are rare, if not non-existent, so you had better be prepared to take something out with you. If unused, it is no problem to throw it in the suitcase and bring it back home. Whether taking rods for beach or boat, whether they are borrowed from a friend or your own beloved property, you will want to protect them. Not only from damage, but from the extremely nifty fingers in operation at airports, hotels and around crowds. Two things will protect your rods while in transit between countries. The best is a piece of four inch plastic drainpipe cut in a length of 6ft 2in. On one end is glued a fixed cap, on the other a sliding cap; screw on a cap or something which can be chained and/or padlocked. Put your name and address on the outside, making sure it is folded over and not visible for all the burglars who frequent airport departure lounges, looking for baggage addresses that tell them you are going on holiday for a week or two. If you haven't thought about it before, now is the time to tape your baggage labels so nobody sees them.

Unfortunately, as a professional angler/writer I take not only the kitchen sink, but half my photography equipment as well. I'm usually overweight, and the plastic drainpipe, although very secure, is a bit on the heavy side. I now use the inside of a commercial roll of floor carpet, which is compressed, reinforced cardboard, and can be obtained, usually free, from a carpet shop. Cut this to the 6ft 2in length which allows for beachcaster sections. Tape a piece of cardboard firmly over one end using masking tape, then when you've got your rods in, tape another piece of cardboard or plastic over the other end. It is a fixture of course, so maybe if you don't have too many rods, you can shove some tee shirts or socks down the tube to stop the blanks rattling around. Keep a roll of tape with you, because customs officers at the other end may want you to cut it open to see inside. If you take reels and they are over 30 lb class I take them in a small grip bag as hand baggage. I would rather do that, than risk them going amiss in transit, besides which it keeps your weight down overall. If you are close, or slightly overweight, take your partner's passport and ticket, then get her to sit away in a corner with all the hand baggage. What the booking handler doesn't see, the excess payment can't get. Try not to get stroppy if you are caught with an excess baggage claim, as they are entitled to weigh your hand baggage as well if they want to. I keep a spring balance in my grip bag, and if you are allowed the usual 20kg baggage allowance, I pack both suitcases to around 22kg. If you lay the rod tube on the scales it often touches both sides of the machine and doesn't register. I personally keep my trolling lures with me, but they should be OK in the suitcase. Wrap them in a sock to stop them getting shattered when the cases are thrown about.

Most cars takes a 6ft 2in rod tube, including desperate taxi drivers by putting it in through the front door, sliding to the opposite rear corner, then easing the rest across the dashboard. If you take a fishing knife for cutting bait, put it in the suitcase as the security men will only take it away from you before you get on the plane. They give you a receipt and tell you to collect it when you disembark, but I always forget myself, and thus lose another good knife. If you have some big shark hooks, put a mask on the points. I once had an argument with a security officer in the States who said a 12/0 Mustad Sea Demon hook was a dangerous weapon and I could use it aggressively. I tried to explain to him that I would have great difficulty in trying to hijack a plane with two marlin lures attached to the hooks, but as he had a magnum on his hip and a mean look in his eye the conversation was very one-sided!

Always ensure you have an adequate tackle insurance that covers you on a worldwide basis. Big reels are expensive, and it will pay you to consult your broker to see if it can be extended cover through your existing household insurance. If you take your own cameras, take note that the X-ray machines on most airport security checks are only safe up to 1000 ASA film. If you have an ASA higher than that, or you are uprating a lower ASA film, then ask for a manual hand search. I get this anyway, as high X rays will fog a colour film completely, and nobody will ever believe you caught that marlin.

As for providing for the weather, I take a light, folding rain mac, and, obviously, sun oil. As a general guide if you have a good tan anyway you can use a factor 4 oil or cream. That means simply that you can stay out in the sun 4 times longer than you would without any protection at all. If you want a bit of a tan, but want to minimise burning, use at least a factor 8 oil or cream, and if you don't even want to go pink, and safeguard yourself against any chance of skin cancer, (the rate is climbing at present) then use at the very least a factor 15. The Berkley company market their Berkley Blockaid which is designed specifically for fishermen, and will not taint any fishing bait if you get it on your fingers. Take also a lip salve/sunscreen, as cracked and bleeding lips are not a pleasant by-product of a day in the hot sun. Put the sun cream on your throat as well, because the harmful rays will bounce up off the surface of the sea, and burn you more efficiently than you would back on dry land. The air is also clearer at sea, with no air pollution to filter the rays.

As for my advice on tackle, I can only tell you the different makes in rod and reel that are probably the best to take, or if you haven't got your own, the best to borrow. For rods few will beat the Conoflex series and North Western for classy, powerful blanks. If you are shore fishing you will want a two piece twelve foot blank capable of throwing three ounces with ease. Take some bomb leads as well. For the boat, again North Western have a super range of carbon/kevlar blanks that are very good for bottom fishing for rays, or heavy fishing from piers when after big fish. On the boat you can really do no better than the Fenwick blanks. They are tried and tested over a number of years, and really can handle those big fish. I have them, and I think you'll find most of the charter boats have them. If possible ensure they have the AFTCO roller guides to reduce line friction and wear. If they have a stainless AFTCO Unibutt, curved or straight, so much the better.

With reels, I have no hesitation in recommending the top two manufacturers, Shimano and Penn International. The Shimano Triton trolling series have 200% more drag surface than most reels and the drag is so silky smooth it is a dream to use. I have nothing but good things to say about them, but they have yet to stand the test of time. Penn Internationals have for years been the battle wagons of most anglers, and take an incredible hammering without letting you down. Either of these two are the best. For shore fishing either the new Shimano fixed spool reels like the baitrunner are sufficient, or the Abu cardinals, similar in appearance. For casting out a heavier bait from the shore, the RYOBI S320 is the tool for the job. Only a star drag reel, but with a good line capacity, it has the strength and large handle to add the power in bringing to shore a big ray or similar bottom species. Good too is the Shimano TLD 20 lever drag reel, but it is better suited to inshore trolling. As for line, I personally use ANDE monofilament, and it has yet to let me down.

Sampo swivels are the top quality swivel snaps, and the best trolling hooks are made by Mustads. For rigging your marlin lures use the Mustad 7731 Sea Demon series, and for regular sharking use the Mustad Seamaster. Both types will benefit from a good sharpening. When shore fishing you will need some spoons or spinners. Many are simply too light to cast well, so try the Ryobi Odin series of wobblers that cast like a bullet and are real fish producers. Good also, are the redgills when fished on a five foot trace. For pilchard oil you can purchase a bulk bottle from Brent's of Hailsham, Station road, Hailsham, Sussex, and use it for both shore groundbaiting, and sharking. There is no need to take things like a flying gaff, as invariably the boat will have that aboard. I find it best to write to the boat owners first asking them specifically what they supply and what is included within the charter price, which then allows you to cut down considerably on the things you think you need. You probably will still end up like me though, taking far more than you can ever use, and complain all the time about how much weight you have to lug around!